Dancing With The Devil
On the Other Side of Freedom

DANCING WITH THE DEVIL
On the Other Side of Freedom
By R. Douglas Veer

Changed Lives Publishing, LLC

2019

First Printing: 2019
ISBN-13: 978-1-7323243-0-5
Library of Congress Control Number: 2019936240

Cover Design: K. Veer
Front Cover Photos: Devil In Flames
Courtesy Pexels.com
Hands of the Prisoner: Adobe Stock Photos
Back Cover Prison Photo: Clint Burton of
BrooklineConnection.com

* * * * * * *

Book Ordering: Amazon.com
Booking Information, please contact:
Doug@DougVeer.com or
Kathy@KathyVeer.com

Changed Lives Publishing, LLC
Region of Augusta, Georgia

PREFACE

In this wonderful country,
the United States of America,
which I love and did fight for
through my military service,
we have been misled by the Judicial System.
We have been raised to believe that in a court of law
we are innocent until proven guilty.

It's not true.

The fact is, the exact opposite is true as was proven by
the recent Brett Kavanaugh hearings.
Never-the-less, this is the greatest
country in the world.

As for me, I was caught in this web of false beliefs
and went to prison an innocent man,
though deemed guilty.

Maybe you've found yourself standing
in the same shoes at one time or another.
Perhaps you will find a bit of yourself in these pages.

ACKNOWLEDGMENTS

I'd like to express my appreciation to the following people:

First, thank you to my wonderful Mom, known affectionately by everyone in our little town as *Ma Veer*. Even in a big family like ours, Mom's love was always *unchanging*. Mom is gone now but I still would like to say, "Thanks Mom, for teaching me that showing love and kindness is the only acceptable way of life. And thanks for teaching me to tie my shoes."

We didn't often wear shoes in the summer, but we did in the winter, and for special occasions. It was in the corner of an old country kitchen near a potbellied stove, that Mom taught me to tie my shoelaces and get ready for the Salvation Army church bus, every Sunday morning, without fail!

Proverbs 22:6 says, ***"Train up a child in the way he should go: and when he is old, he will not depart from it,"*** (KJV). For me, it all started right there, sitting in the corner tying my laces, so I could go to church.

Thanks also to my Dad, whom I don't remember ever staying home from work, even when he was sick. By that he taught me the importance of a strong work ethic that I've carried all these years; it has become ingrained into my very character.

Third, thanks to my eight brothers and five sisters who saw the worst of me during my *wild* years, yet still loved me and forgave me just like Mom taught us.

Fourth, thanks to Mom and Dad Ronson, whom I met during their later years of ministry. In those days I was struggling to know right from wrong and live accordingly. I *so* wanted to leave behind my years of disobedience. They became my spiritual teachers and living examples of Christ, so I say, "Thank you, Mom and Dad Ronson for being the second set of parents I needed so much."

Fifth, I want to offer many, many, thanks to my children. They often allowed me to be a weak and foolish man; one who made many mistakes in life. Through it all, however, they continued to bless me with the sweetest words on earth: *"Daddy, I love you."*

Above all, I am very grateful to the most wonderful Daddy there will ever be--my Savior and Lord, Jesus Christ. Allow me to repeat part of an essay written in school by my daughter, Amanda. The essay was called, *Parents Are Heroes*. Let this portion of it be my prayer:

"Thank you, oh Lord, my Savior;
You're not only the best Daddy
of them all; You're my Hero too."
(Amanda Faith Veer)

--Sincerely . . . R. Douglas Veer

INTRODUCTION

THERE'S NOTHING BETTER THAN FREEDOM

This book--in part--is about how I ended up in a real prison, behind real iron bars. But I also describe different *kinds* of prisons: those with concrete and steel walls, and those with no walls at all, yet they are very much prisons, indeed.

Of course, just the sight of a prison with its cold metal doors and dismal surroundings would cause anyone to fear. That's because it's where you could be held captive knowing it would not be easy to get out.

To think of it another way, prisons are made *by* man and *for* man because of his crimes. But even worse is that after a man has paid the price for his wrong-doings and is released, he may continue to be imprisoned in some other way.

For example, a drug addict on the street, who commits crimes or sells his or her body to pay for another chemical high, is in a prison of his own weakness. Or, a person may be in bondage to alcohol, food, money, sex, or power. Today, people find themselves in all kinds of prisons such as self-loathing, depression, physical or sexual abuse, uncontrollable anger, fear, guilt, or a myriad of other emotional bondages. The list seems endless.

Yes, many folks do in fact exist in one kind of prison or another, and it may seem easier to open a steel door to freedom than to work through a gripping personal problem that locks a person down. Many who have left physical bars behind are still searching for *real* freedom and never find it.

I've been locked away behind thick walls and razor wire fences, but I've also been entrapped by other things. Now that I'm free, I'm doing all I can to help others inside and outside of physical prisons.

The ministry God has given me includes visiting convicted prisoners and their families and sharing Jesus Christ with them. Once they are on the outside, and free from their confinement, we try to help ex-inmates find employment and housing and help them find a sense of self-worth through community support.

Also, through local, social, and church programs, we minister to the families, especially to the children. To further help families we also offer Biblical counseling for marriage and pre-marital situations, and we help children who are in troubled homes, especially where one or both parents are facing a criminal sentence.

IT IS A SPIRITUAL MATTER

Now, let me get to the heart of it. Being in or out of jail has nothing to do with being truly free. I'm convinced that the deeper problem that robs people of their freedom is spiritual. That's the crux of it and it is of great concern to me.

After I was released, I used to say, "There's nothing better than freedom". With all my heart, I still believe that, but now, I've come to realize there's a fuller, three-dimensional aspect to freedom: the physical, the emotional, and the spiritual. But the power to be free from *every* kind of prison exists only in the spiritual realm, and that strength can only be found through a personal relationship with Jesus Christ.

It's like this: Jesus is your attorney. He's ready to go before God Almighty on your behalf. He's ready to go to the highest court in Heaven and plead *His* innocence for *you*. And not only that, He's already paid the price for you to be free! All you have to do is accept it and faithfully walk in it.

I've enjoyed all kinds of freedoms, but most of all, I have rested in that real freedom that only comes from intimately knowing my Savior. He has released me from an actual prison, but also from drugs, alcohol, sin and even death. He has given me eternal life. He has set me free to be the person He created me to be. He has placed a call upon my life to help others find their way. And even though I am just a simple man, with human weaknesses, He has given me the ability and the power to fulfill that call.

WHAT ABOUT YOU?

Spiritual freedom through Jesus Christ will free you too. You can walk away from every kind of prison you can imagine. Even if you're in a prison cell, as I was, you can become completely liberated! Yes, God wants to work with you, exactly the way you are, and exactly where you are. He fully understands even the smallest detail about your life. He created you, and He wants the best for you.

When you give your heart to Him, He will immediately begin working out His plan. Then, as you learn, and grow, you'll begin to see that you're free indeed, and you'll be on your way to becoming as complete a person as you can be.

Since I found freedom in Jesus Christ, He has done much more for me than I could have ever dreamed. For one thing, He's allowed me the great joy of seeing several family members come to Him, including:

My Mother - born again October 12th, 1980
at 71 years old.
Both my youngest precious daughters,
Amanda Faith Veer - born again July 19th, 1989
at 10 years old, and
Hope Ronson Veer - born again July 9th, 1990
at 9 years old,
and there were several others.

If you don't have Christ in your life as your Lord and Savior, then I hope as you read this book, you'll come and add your name to this list. If you do, your name will also be written on that great list in Heaven called the "Lamb's Book of Life!"

Salvation is about a relationship with Christ, and it is the only way you'll ever have that *real* freedom I'm talking about. Without this freedom, you'll always be in bondage to your weak, destructive behaviors. They're real, and they're strong. Don't wait another day or even another moment. Give your heart and life to the Lord right now, will you? It's just this simple:

THE SINNER'S PRAYER

"Lord Jesus, I know that I'm a sinner and I'm so sorry that I can't overcome that by myself. Without You, it's useless for me to even try but with Your help, I'll do all I can to follow You and Your example.

Thank You for dying on the cross in my place and shedding Your blood for my sins. I accept that gift right now. Lord Jesus, please come into my heart and cleanse me of all my sins.I receive You as my Savior. Please help me to obediently live for You, from this moment on.

I trust that Your Word is true according to what the Bible says. Thank You. I do pray this in the name of Jesus Christ. Amen."

I hope you prayed this prayer and meant it. If you have, you will come to see God richly bless you with His freedom and His great love.

CHAPTER ONE

THE CELL DOOR

CLAAANG-G-G !-!-! The heavy iron cell door slammed shut in my face, leaving a rude, ugly ringing sound in the air as I've never heard before. It had me shut in where the air was dark, the room was hot and dry, and the smell was inescapable. The stink was caused by too many bodies crammed into too small of a space.

The mocking ring echoed it's cruel laughter in my ears. "For everrr . . . for everrr . . . for everrr," clutching me with its awful, fearful tentacles wrapped tightly around my mind and heart. I thought I would never again feel the cool breeze, freely dancing across my face.

Here I was. Nothing in this world had ever torn so deeply at my emotions. It wasn't so much the actual slamming of the door. Rather, it was the very air, vibrating with a heavy, hellish death cry that went on and on inside that hollow, hateful "Claaang-g-g . . . ." It vibrated through every fiber of my being.

With my fingers gripping those filthy bars, I imagined I could open the *iron-ribbed monster* that had just robbed me of my freedom. I could see myself walking out of there, but the clangorous laughter went on and on with its never-ending taunting message.

Then, in that same moment--with the noise still ringing--my conscious mind said, "Man, you'll probably never know freedom again." Then it hit me. I was probably standing in the exact place where I would draw my very last breath. Reality struck. It was here. It was literally up close and in my face.

Panic swept over me and I tightened my grip. My life was about to drastically change and it scared me. I realized that if I did die in here, it would probably happen when I was all alone. I'd have no one to care for me, no one to understand me, no one to comfort me, no one to share my passing from this life.

THE OTHER SIDE OF FREEDOM

There's fear in loneliness, and there's loneliness in fear. I had both. I was in my late 40s so there was no way I'd be able to out-live a maximum sentence of 27 years in this cage of wild animals. I was on the other side of freedom, and I wondered if I would ever leave this dark, stinking cell, or would it be, "For everrr . . . for everrr . . . for everrr . . . locked away for everrr!"

I stared in unbelief at the encrusted, chipped, gray paint on the bars. It was like being transported millions of miles away into some foreign universe, far from anything that resembled normal life.

I slid my finger along the flat horizontal plate that held the upright bars together. I was disgusted. Grime covered everything. The thought of it all caused a deep fear from somewhere inside of me to well up. "Am I really in this repulsive place? Am I *really* behind prison bars? Maybe it's just a dream and I'll wake up soon. . ."

My mind waded through images of tough, dangerous, hardened men; men to be feared; men consumed by that certain element of human depravity that was spawned in a place such as this. Such men knew in the depths of their souls that this was all there was ever going to be. They had nothing to lose, so why obey the rules? Why bother being decent?

2

Was I going to become one of *them?* Or would I end up becoming a *victim* of one of them? Is this what my life had finally come to? Prison? Was my freedom gone? What happens now?

Then, out of nowhere, my ears were filled with the most pain wracked scream I'd ever heard: "G-O-O-O-D-D-D! Where are you?! Are you in here? Please help me!!" The sound rang its way down through the dark corridors. Then I realized it was my own voice crying out into this unfeeling, godforsaken place.

My chest was tight with panic. My breath was caught in my lungs, hanging there like a lead ball, moving neither up nor down. Heat spread across my brow and slowly warmed my cheeks, while a cold fever broke over my face. I was panting like a wild dog. I wanted to vomit. One knot after another formed in the pit of my stomach.

The facts washed over me again. My silent thoughts told me, "This is *real,*" and I wanted the dream to be over. I wanted it to end! But then, I heard that scream again."G-O-O-O-D-D-D! Where are you?! Are you in here?" The words hovered in the air like dust particles. The empty voices bounced between the cold concrete walls, convincing me that I was not dreaming; this was a living nightmare! I was locked away somewhere, in a place outside of reach. I was confined behind steel, and there was no way out. Yes. Even grown men cry.

INDIAN SUMMERS PAST

As a boy, I grew up in the mid-western plains states, where life was simple. There was nothing much to see on the horizon except flat, grassy land for miles and miles and more miles. So, my summer days and my Indian summer nights were often spent searching that far, distant horizon, hoping something interesting might exist out there. I knew there were massive mountains, somewhere, and great, green, dense forests, and huge blue lakes and rivers filled with beautiful, cool, flowing waters. I knew the expanse of the great oceans would be unending, almost as if they were denying any world existed beyond them. Surely Columbus and his crew must have felt that sense of awe too, as they searched for this great land of ours.

But now, like a dying Indian lifting his voice, crying out across the hills toward his homeland, the pained-filled voice bellowed out into the darkness of the prison: "Freeedddooommm! Give me my freeedddooommm!!"

My voice paled temporarily, hoping for an answer, only to hear a mocking response: "No more . . . no more . . . no more . . . no more freedom . . . ha-ha-ha!"

I was yearning for those childhood days once again. I wanted to go back to those hours I spent lying beneath a tree, thinking about what could be out across the horizon and beyond. My heart searched for that elusive reality of life as I knew it. But the blasphemous echo resounded again, saying, "Hey! Here it is, dummy! This is what's out there! No blue skies, no green hills, just this miserable cell. Get used to it."

Standing there, holding on to the bars with clenched fists I thought, "No man has ever suffered as much as this. No other man has ever felt this much loneliness and pain so far away from his home.

Then I thought of Jesus. He was arrested too. Oh, and He had a beard just like me. But He was beaten, spit on, and attacked. The guards ripped His beard out by the hand full, and he was tortured, laughed at, and nailed to a cross. He died there. And yes, He was far from His home too, but He did it willingly, just because of me. Who was I to complain?

The incessant never-ending noise of many voices jumbled together jerked me back to reality. Here I was, inside a stacked tier of iron cages, and just like mine, each foul cell held anguished men with crushed dreams who were longing for days gone by.

I gazed into the semi-darkness. I wanted to see those rolling hills. I wanted to sit in the meadow and let my eyes wander through mountains and forests, imagining it all in my mind's eye. Instead, my soul wept. I felt like a great lion that had wandered off by itself across the dry Serengeti Desert, old and waiting to die.

Again, I wanted this dream to be over. My heart cried, "freeedddooommm!" But the silence proved that no answer would find me. I continued to wait patiently but hopelessness forced me to fall to the chilled floor in defeat, here in this prison of "foreverness".

CHAPTER TWO

MY POOR FAMILY

I don't know if any of my thirteen brothers and sisters had ever been locked up but I can say, without embarrassment, that although I was raised in a very poor family we were never poor in love. The giving and receiving of our love was full and rich. We had so much affection in our household that you couldn't have afforded to buy it with all the money in the world!

My upbringing made me a strong person, perhaps too strong in a way. When you come from a family of fourteen children, you learn to live by your wits. You also learn that whoever shows the most anger usually gets what he wants, and if you don't fight for what you want, you grow up being a wimp. That was something I didn't want to be.

I guess I got my character from my Daddy. He was a strong person; a full-blooded Kraut, bearing all the traits of an iron-willed German Father. He considered discipline the primary ingredient in raising children. I guess that philosophy passed on down to me because I have carried those same attitudes into my adult life.

Admittedly though, for years I had been much too hard on my kids. I always punished them for misbehaving or breaking the rules. Back then I didn't realize that *punishment* only satisfies one's own anger and frustration, while *discipline* is what helps children learn, and grow into loving, caring persons.

I finally do see the difference. Being an over-bearing, disciplinarian only caused my family relationships to suffer. I wish I would have understood this sooner.

In defense of my Dad, however, I will say this: he had his hands full with us kids. The fourteen of us were a great responsibility riding on his shoulders. He couldn't afford to put up with our foolishness. Never-the-less Dad was a living example to our family; a real working man who spent his whole life *on the job* as our provider.

THE GREAT DEPRESSION

When my dad was a young husband and Father in his mid-twenties, he carried us through the Great Depression. A few years later, he saw us through World War II. We finally made it into the 1950s when times became much better. I don't know how Mom and Dad managed but we always had enough, and we always knew we were loved. And we had God on our side along with some plain old American grit.

Here's a poem I wrote many years ago, about my family:

IN MEMORY OF . . .

Our table was set poorly;
our shoes were thin and bare.
The winds blew cold upon our heads
protected just by hair.
The clothes we wore were patch on patch
from years of hand-me-downs.
Yes, we were the poorest of the poor
that lived here in this town.

The rich kids sneered and laughed at us;
the poor kids turned their backs.
'Cause we came from the "Organ Factory"
down by the railroad tracks.

But Daddy always worked each day
so we could learn the same.
And he was never shamed like me
when he said, "Veer's my name".

And as the years went on
I could see that Daddy gave me pride,
and taught me honesty and trust
and compassion too, besides.
He taught me strength and warmth and love
and kindness for the weak.
He taught me to know right from wrong
and showed me how to seek . . .

. . . the richer things that life can give
to those who take the time
to search out and to reach for life
instead of being blind,
to all the goodness that there is;
to reap, as we love on,
instead of reaching for money
and what to spend it on.

Our table was set poorly;
our shoes were thin and bare.
But Daddy fed us love and kindness
and we grew, with food to spare.
Food of love and decency
that we can give to all.
That's why our Daddy's table made us grow
to be ten feet tall.
                    --R.D. Veer

A GLIMPSE OF HEAVEN

When I was young, mom used to send us kids to the Salvation Army Church, but when I was about 10 or 11 years old, we switched over to the Church of the Nazarene. Both places are indelibly etched in my mind.

I'll never forget those Sunday mornings. One of my fondest memories was in our old country kitchen behind the pot-bellied wood stove where Mama helped me tie my shoes. It seemed like I was "all thumbs" while everyone else was already scurrying out the door. There was always a mad rush to get ready as Mama dressed us and put us on the church bus.

That brings up another thought. It's funny how a simple thing like *shoes* can unlock a memory.

I remember going to a church Christmas party one year when I was about eight. We were all leaving the lobby of the Senate Hotel, where the party had been held, and a little girl our age was suddenly hit by a car. I don't know what happened to the girl but there in the street, in front of the building, she was hit so hard that she was pulled right out of her shoes, and they were left on the pavement where she had been standing.

I'm not sure why that impressed me so, but I guess it made me think about Heaven and such things. It seemed to me, even back then, that when folks die and go to Heaven they leave everything behind, just like she left her shoes.

SUNDAY SCHOOL

As a young boy, I thought a lot about spiritual things and often remembered what I'd learned in Sunday School, like the story of Jacob's ladder, and Joseph's coat of many colors. I remembered the dream he had about the many sheaves of grain that bowed down to the one. I remembered stories about Noah's Ark, and stories about Jesus when He was a boy, just like me. Those Bible stories stayed on my mind during the long church-bus rides home. (Please realize that if you'll give them the chance, your children will get more out of Sunday school than you will ever know.)

Then, when we'd get home, we'd come off the bus clamoring through the kitchen door like a bunch of wild Indians. We'd be waving our exciting, colorful reports, and blurting out all we had learned as we were seated around the table Mom had so lovingly prepared.

Mom always made a delicious Sunday meal with homemade noodles and chicken and mashed potatoes and gravy. It reminded me that one day Jesus is going to prepare a great feast for us in Heaven and I thought, "There'll be lots of people at that table too, and lots of gravy to dip our bread in!" No, it won't be wine; we never had wine in our house. But that was okay Mom's great dinners made me look forward to *The Last Supper* or *The Marriage Supper of the Lamb*. (As a young--ever-hungry boy--I always had the two suppers confused.)

While my facts were a little mixed up, those Sunday School lessons made a lifelong impression on me. Please know that today's children can have those wonderful memories too, and they will benefit greatly from what they learn in church if you take them. They need to have those kinds of influences in their lives instead of growing up on massive diets of violent movies, and video games. Give them a chance, and you'll see that it will give them unseen strength to live in this crazy, wild, messed up world. You'll be thankful you did.

IT TAKES A FAMILY

Being in a close-knit family is also very important. What are children going to learn by going out after church to burger joints and the like? They're filled with noise and poor attitudes. Rudeness is often on display, and everything is "hurry, hurry, hurry". Can we really show a child a sense of family in such an atmosphere? Can a child associate those places with Heaven?

If our lives don't portray godliness or "heavenliness", what will our kids have to tie them to purity and kindness as they grow into adulthood? Have we failed our children today with our modern lifestyles? No, Mrs. Hillary Clinton, it doesn't take a village, it takes a family! It takes a home life filled with the love of a Mom and Dad, and a home with a clear cut example of Christ, lived out each day. That's what children need but are often robbed of. No wonder the world is a mess.

Today, T.V. characters serve as role models for family relationships, and that covers everything from the ridiculous to the violent. Television characters have overshadowed *real* family values, and without *those values*, where can our children find good examples to live by?

I'm so glad my young life was filled with family and church. At 12 years old, I joined the Salvation Army band which became like another family to me. Just from the examples set by the people who were there, I received profitable teaching that later carried me through some of the roughest times of my life. *Seeds* were planted that led me to pursue decency, respect, and kindness. And those seeds grew to maturity, helping me weather many storms.

I'm afraid the same opportunities are becoming quite scarce for many of our young people today. Home life is lacking; sometimes church life too, and definitely the school environment. How sad that is to recognize and admit.

CHAPTER THREE

A TIME OF MEASURING VALUES

I have always liked cars. I guess that's why I spent so much time playing with them in the dirt under the front porch. I bought my first *real* car when I was only 15 years old. It was a rough looking old 1946 Plymouth convertible that I purchased from a man I'd never met before. I didn't have an adult to help me buy it, I barely knew how to drive, and I had no drivers license, so I did the best I could.

Yes, life was *interesting* back then. In those days, I was already living on my own. Why? Because by the time I had reached the age of 14, I was hard-headed and difficult to deal with. So I left home and took up residence in a rooming house. I worked after school in a meat market to support myself, and when that business closed at 9:00 in the evening, I went on to my other job, setting pins in the downtown bowling alley. (Bowling alleys were not automated back then!)

Anyway, back to the car story. I found this car that I really liked, and my friend, Wesley Biedler, went with me to look at it. The car was long and sleek, and absolutely gorgeous! At least it was to me.

I bought it, and drove it, (without a license), and boy, did I love that car . . . that is . . . until 30 minutes later when it started to rain. With Wesley's help, we figured out how to put the top up, but we might as well have left it down because there wasn't enough cloth on it to make a good pair of blue jeans. And the rain poured in!

Drenched to the skin, I made my way back to the seller and told the man I didn't want the car. He told me, "Boy, ya' bought it and it's yours! I didn't make ya' no promises an' ya' didn't ask no questions. Ya' were real happy when ya' left here, so it's yours now. Git outta here!"

Standing there in tears, I didn't know what to do. Only one thing came to mind, so I said, "I'm gonna tell my Daddy that you cheated me, and he'll make you do me right!"

With an air of ugly sarcasm the man sneered at me, "Oh yeah? Well just who is yer Daddy anyway, big boy?"

I told him, "Bill Veer is my Dad and he knows all about cars and . . ."

The man interrupted me. "Oh . . . So you're Bill Veer's boy? Well hey, yeah! Just hold on a minute. Sure, I'll uh . . . I'll give you your money back, son."

That day I learned a valuable life lesson. I learned that a person's reputation is everything and my Dad was living proof of that. In the Bible, we're told that a good reputation is worth more than silver or gold, and that wisdom is *better* than gold. Now, when the devil tries to cheat me, I can stand and declare to him, "Hey. I'll tell my Daddy on you!" He might reply, "Which Daddy is that?" And I'll tell him, "My Daddy, Jesus."

So now I always try to remember to transfer my trust over to my "Heavenly Dad". Why? Because He's more powerful, more caring, more loving, and more valuable to me than anything in this world. There's no other Daddy like Him.

We can fill our lives to the brim with expensive things, but the wisest investment we will ever make is to put God first. Then, after we've done our part, He'll handle the rest. He'll take care of us, and never leave us nor forsake us for any reason.

Do I still like convertibles? Well, of course. Even though I was disappointed with my first one, I've had several others over the years. They are still *the apple of my eye!*

TURNING POINT

For a moment, my mind wandered away from the hellish prison cell, and I thought about how I would love to be that young teenager again. Back then life was uncomplicated, and despite my lack of control over things, it was predictable. I went to school, had a couple of jobs, had friends, and dreamed of going into the Navy. I went with the flow of life, and everything worked out alright. Well, for the most part anyway.

Okay, so I missed going to college right out of High School, which would have been nice. And I always hoped to find someone wise, like a mentor, who would tuck me up under his wing and guide and direct me, but that blessing alluded me. Even so, the early years were pretty good to me.

The only real trauma I remember during my younger years was getting very sick just before I turned 16 years old. I contracted hepatitis C, which left me extremely weak and I spent several months in the hospital. In fact, I guess I slipped into a coma for a while, but by the grace of God, I came through it.

I was finally released with the understanding that my diet would have to be completely fat-free for the rest of my life or I would have a relapse. Even eating potato chips was out of the question for me because of the grease content.

Mom and Dad thought it would be best for me to go live on the farm with my oldest brother Bill, and his wife Charity. They thought I'd recover better there, so off I went, taking the doctor's rules and regulations with me. I would have to maintain a fruit and vegetable diet, and I could not do any physical exercise.

Well, so much for that! My brother's father-in-law, Ralph, had been a cook by trade, and he had a whole different slant on things. Every day, after my brother and his wife left for work--and the coast was clear--Ralph got busy with me.

First, he would cook a *Grand Slam* breakfast! That included toast, eggs over easy, sausage or bacon, and milk or orange juice. Pretty low-fat, huh? For lunch, I might get some nice sliced tomatoes, fried potatoes, pork chops or a hamburger patty with luscious-tasting grease drippings. Mmm! I can still taste it today. But for supper, when Chat and Bill were home to see what was going on, I received only a plate of fruit and vegetables.

Additionally, after breakfast, Ralph would take me outside to the woodpile and give me a double-bit ax to split firewood. He worked me for two or three hours at a time! And then, when that was done, I'd have to carry it all by the armload, down to the basement!

Oh yeah. That was some rest and relaxation, right? I did not get to lay around on a pillow and watch TV. I guess Ralph could have been the death of me, but as he fed me, and he worked me, he would say,

"Those stupid doctors. They don't know nothin'. What you need is good food, fresh air, and hard work to build you into a man! Stick with me boy and I'll make you strong again." And believe me, that's what he did!

The months passed on from February to October, and we had the doctors really scratching their heads. I was supposed to be a 75 pound weakling for the rest of my days, but instead, I gained weight and muscle, and by the middle of November 1954, I was 128 pounds and considered physically and emotionally fit to be accepted into the Navy. I had just reached the age of seventeen, and it was a real turning point in my life.

LIFE AT SEA

The icing on the cake for me was my acceptance into submarine school, graduating, and being granted the privilege to serve there. Joining the Navy was one of my better choices. I wish I could say the same for some of the other decisions I made.

In retrospect, many of my other life choices were not so good. For example, a couple of years later, I decided to go A.W.O.L. That was definitely not too bright on my part. How did that happen?

Well, I met the "Devil" in Yokosuka, Japan, in the bars and in the company of alcohol and exciting Japanese women. I forgot everything else as the Saki flowed and the Devil played his music for me to dance to. There on the stupid side of freedom, everything else left my mind and my common sense.

One particular night, I didn't return to the boat, (the submarine), and I stayed out for three more nights and mornings. When I came to my senses--fearing punishment--I headed back to the boat. I was charged and had to go to "Captains Mast", a court of my peers in which the Captain of my boat sentenced me to two months in a Marine brig, run by Marines who didn't care too much for Sailors.

I spent many of my days in the brig working, along side other offenders. We were given sledgehammers, picks, and shovels, and taken out to the air-strip to break up the concrete. It took me a while to get over that experience. But on the plus side, my 130 pounds became a hardened 180 pounds of muscle, so it was good for me.

You see, back then I was motivated by my flesh, so I made decisions outside of Christ, and drew only on my own limited strength. My physical and emotional senses were my guide instead of allowing the Spirit of God to lead me. I've so wished I could go back and correct all my wrongs. I'm sure I'm not alone in feeling this way. Many other people probably feel the same way about their lives and about their past decisions. Sadly though, by the time we realize it, it can be too late.

CHAPTER FOUR

POOR CHOICES

My military résumé may impress some folks, but if anyone really looked at my life, they would have seen all my failures.

For example, I chose the wrong schools and turned down ones that really could have enhanced my life later on. Because of my very high IQ, I was offered NAVCAD, (a Naval Aviation Cadet Program in Norman Oklahoma). I had also been invited to OCS, (Officers Candidate School on the east coast). Actually, the door was open to the school of my choice.

Well, I didn't accept either of the first two offers because I thought the programs were about a year long, and I wanted to get started on becoming whatever being a sailor was all about. Sadly, I learned years later that NAVCAD and OCS were only 12-week programs and I would have received the E-5 pay-rate instead of the E-1 Seaman recruit pay-rate. How I wish I would have had someone to advise me.

As a kid, my older brother-in-law, Dutch--whom I greatly admired--was a cook on submarines. I decided to follow in his footsteps so I went to commissary school in San Diego for about 4 months. Then after a short leave at home, I went on to submarine school in New London, Connecticut.

I was sent to Hawaii for my first submarine assignment. I deployed aboard the "K-2", a sub-killer type of submarine with major sonar capabilities that could track and destroy other submarines.

After several months on the K-2, I transferred to the "U.S.S. Stickleback SS-415". During that time we made several cruises to the Far East. The mission proved to be a dangerous venture due to the life and death perils we faced, sneaking into places we shouldn't have been. The Stickleback now sleeps in about 1,800 fathoms, (nearly 11,000 feet) of water in the Pacific Ocean.

Looking back on these frequent secret expeditions, I felt pretty special. Those experiences were good for me; they helped me mature.

The Navy took me all over the world, but God kept me safe. When the other servicemen were contracting heartaches and venereal diseases, God protected me from those things too. He kept me morally decent and pure at that stage of my life. While other men were getting what the world had to offer, I spent my time writing to my dream girl back home. She was the one I finally gave my heart to. Before too long, I gave myself to her in marriage. I'll tell you more about that later.

So when it was time for me to be discharged, I had the option to extend my service for six more years. It was a tremendous offer because it would have included a two-year college degree, followed by two years in Nuclear Fission school, and two years of active military service. That could have led to several other very beneficial possibilities. For one thing, I would have been at the half-way mark for the twenty years required for full retirement. I could have retired as a Navy career man, but I turned it down. You see . . . my wife, Judy, wanted me out of the service, so I left.

Many factors worked against me as a young man. Poor decision making followed me beyond my Navy days. I often ended up working at the wrong kinds of jobs due to a lack of education. Also, I made some really poor and damaging, relationship choices. One of those choices that severely impacted me was my decision to marry while I was still in the service.

To sum it all up, I would say that after getting out of the Navy, I had a lot of hardships in my early twenties and it was only a foreshadow of the troubled life to come.

GETTING BY IN TIGHT PLACES

I mentioned earlier that as a young boy of five or six years old, I loved to play with my little cast iron cars and trucks. I would play under the front porch where I built roads and bridges for them in the dirt. Somehow I found comfort there; that spot served as my refuge. And though I felt rather confined, it served as a foundation, too, for experiences I would find myself in, later on in life.

So one day, at the beginning of first grade, I had refused to go to school. I was actually on my way to school when my older brother started teasing me about my *girlfriend*. (Her name was Ana Lea Foshua.) I got so embarrassed about it that I ran all the way back home and hid inside my *refuge*.

Years later, I again found myself in small, enclosed spaces, yet I felt secure and protected. One of those tight spots was, of course, being on a submarine. Even though I went on some hair-raising missions, I thought our enemy was at a disadvantage because they could never find us. In spite of those dangerous assignments and close calls, I loved submarines and never wanted to leave. I would have stayed had my wife not demanded that I give it up.

After I left the Navy I went into construction work, which presented more challenges. I had to go underneath houses, or into very tight, confined places, but since I never felt claustrophobic it was natural for me.

ON TOP OF THE WORLD

In my twenties, I traded those tight places for high places. I worked high steel for a while, climbing structures that were 200 or 300 feet in the air, hanging structural beams for tall buildings.

Late one afternoon, near quitting time, I was working inside a steel framework at the top of a building. The workday was shutting down, and the men were heading home, but I was left up there by mistake.

Sometime after the whistle had blown, I was discovered up there, and finally brought down. I guess I was trapped so-to-speak, but I never *felt* trapped. I could have locked my feet into the web of the columns and slid down a floor at a time That would have been a natural thing to do as we often did that to go from one floor to the next. But since it was the end of the day I waited, because I knew *someone* would come and get me.

There's a Bible passage in Hebrews which relates to that. In it, God promises, ***"He will never leave us nor forsake us,"*** (Hebrews 13"5; ESV). I've never been left behind by Him yet. He's been a great comfort to me, even when I've worked hundreds of feet in the air.

People have asked me if I ever felt scared working up so high. But I never was. Being in closets, under cars, in crawl spaces, attics, or high above the ground: these things were never more than minor issues for me.

My off the job experiences were another story. Living in the world with the sort of company I was keeping was much more dangerous. It was a life riddled with drugs and alcohol, and it drove me to the edge of my existence. But having a youthful resilience on my side, I thought life was pretty good; on the surface, I had no complaints. The Devil and his little demons continued to dance with me, and I thought, "all is well".

CHAPTER FIVE

THE WIFE THAT SHOULDN'T HAVE BEEN

Her name was Judy. I met Judith Lynn Moss in February of 1955 when I was on leave from attending boot-camp at Great Lakes Naval Center in Chicago. She lived next door to my brother and his wife, whom I was visiting. They lived in Loves Park, Illinois. (What a name for a city!) And when I noticed her, I asked to meet her. My sister-in-law, Charity, introduced us and wouldn't you know it, the romance was on. Before long, we were engaged.

Looking back on it now, I should have let the whole thing drop, because a few months after we met I asked her to marry me. That was a big mistake. Plans were made for a wedding and I was so happy. But then she sent me a very discouraging letter and that should have been the end of it right then. But it was just the beginning of sorrows for me. Let me explain.

The engagement apparently meant nothing to her. She continued with her free-wheeling lifestyle; she had no apparent regard for me because we weren't married yet. While I was out at sea she sent me a "Dear John" letter, but when her mother found out about it, *she* sent me a *rush telegram* while I was at sea, to make it look as though Judy had a change of heart. The telegram said:

"I WANT YOU, I NEED YOU, I LOVE YOU.
DO NOT READ THE NEXT LETTER YOU GET.
DESTROY IT,
LOVE JUDY."

Needless to say, I was overjoyed; not just because of the telegram, but to get any mail was a

24

thrill, period. Mail was scarce out there in the middle of the ocean.

So when the telegram reached my hand, I was very excited to read it, and of course, I was doubly excited and curious about the *next* letter I *wasn't* supposed to open. And of course, I opened it and read it.

It turned out to be a "Dear John" letter. In it, Judy explained that she couldn't wait for me any longer because she was going with someone else. There it was. The truth was staring me right in the face! I should have accepted it and went on with my life, but I guess it wasn't meant to be. That interfering telegram from her mother had persuaded me to carry on.

Furthermore, Judy's mom thought I was the *finest* young man one could ever want to meet. She *definitely* wanted me to be with her daughter, so she pushed us to go ahead with the wedding, which took place on August 4th, 1957. Let me repeat: the wedding should never have happened.

After three children and more than five years of constant fighting, Judy and I finally came to a breaking point. In December of 1962, our marriage completely fell apart. While I was at work one day, she walked out with another man. She just walked out the door and disappeared. It was something I never believed could have happened, but it did.

She took all our money leaving me one dime. Yes, literally one dime! I hitch-hiked from Albuquerque, New Mexico to Rockford, Illinois to see her once more. But there was no talking to her, so I figured it needed to be called, finished.

Actually, Judy had left me five or six times during our marriage when her mother was living near us, but this was her last time and I believed I should make the separation final. I hated to do it, but our break up utterly devastated me, and since she told me there was no reconciliation possible, and since she had gone back to her mother's home town, halfway across the county, I felt it was the only choice I had left.

After working for a while and making some money to buy a car, I left and went to Houston, Texas, hoping to figure out how to cope with all that had happened. I lived in Houston, mostly to be near my younger sisters Grace and Peachie, and their husbands. I thought a sense of family would help, but still, there was no peace for me.

I was restless and moved back to Illinois. I tried to find Judy and let her know I had decided to file for divorce. I traced every avenue I could only to discover she had moved to New York. Try as I did, I could not pinpoint her actual location, so I made the divorce legal by public notification.

A few years later I learned that at only 29 years old, she died of cancer. I felt a tremendous loss. After all, she was my first real love, but we just couldn't make it work. I missed that perfect, God ordained marriage that I thought I would have forever. How disappointed I was.

ALONE AND FREE

Even with the trauma and heartbreak of it all, I know God was still taking care of me. At the same time, I felt nothing in my life was working out. Just like the popular song describes, I was *alone again, naturally.*

So, I began roaming from place to place, never staying anywhere too long. For a change of pace and a little self-fulfillment, I moved to Dallas and enrolled at the Dallas Art Institute. I had always been pretty good at art and wanted to see how much I could improve; perhaps even make it a career.

Many of the other students were involved in the *Jesus Movement* of the day and I became attracted to it also. But I was just like many uninformed young people of the 60s. I was needy and searching for something real in life. It was a time of "free love" but I didn't know the deeper meaning of the word. To me, love was sensual at its best, and painful when it was bad. I followed the philosophy everyone was living by: "If it feels good, do it". So, if it felt good, I did it! All the while, my heart yearned for more than the world had to offer.

I'm so thankful I wasn't stuck with that understanding. I have since found real love by accepting Jesus Christ as my Savior. I've learned that God's love is everlasting because it's authentic, and it only comes by giving one's heart, to Christ. This kind of love is called "agapé" love and it's based on *giving* instead of selfishly *taking*.

Even back then I believed in Christ's love for me, and it should have satisfied me, but to be honest, the flesh is strong and hard to break away from. Unfortunately, it still had a stronghold on me because I wasn't completely surrendered.

I continued to roam, hoping to find peace of mind and heart. I wanted to be selfishly free, travel, and have *fun in the sun!* I thought that would be the way to shake off the rejection I suffered.

I lived and talked like the generation I was hanging out with: the Hippies of the day. I used to say, "Don't judge me! If you people don't understand my way of life, then you're missing the meaning of *freedom* entirely." If only I had known more about that agapé love Jesus offered. How different my life would have been.

27

FREEDOM TO RUN

The Hippie scene got old, so I started running with a motorcycle gang. That's where I planned my next search for freedom. My vagabond and now immoral lifestyle took me to many places like Colorado Springs, Colorado, Los Angeles, California, Shreveport, Bossier, and New Orleans, all in Louisiana. Little Rock, and Texarkana, Arkansas, Miami, and Cocoa Beach, Florida, Houston, and Galveston, Texas, San Diego, California, Rome, Georgia, Birmingham, Alabama, Illinois, New Mexico, and on and on.

Yeah, I was running in the fast lane but I never would have admitted to anyone how tiresome it got to be. I was having sex for love, yet never feeling the security of belonging. I lacked peace, and contentment and it hurt. The only security I found was *"in the moment"* because I had no assurance of tomorrow. Life for me was empty.

My freedom became foolishness, my foolishness became loneliness, and my loneliness became like a prison sentence. I ran with guys that would nail men to trees in the woods and leave them there, just to square up debts.

Many in the gang were arrested, maimed, or killed, as they filled the emptiness of their lives with drugs. I used *window pane* and *blue dot* acid. I smoked marijuana, hash, and PCP, (also known as Angel Dust) and psilocybin, made from mushrooms, dusted on marijuana joints. I took some of the latest recreational pills such as red hearts, black beauties, and other "speed" drugs. But thankfully, I bypassed the extremes, like using needles and snorting cocaine. I know the providential hand of God had to have been on me because amazingly, I survived. There is no other explanation.

I was always searching but never finding what I was looking for. The good things in life alluded me, like trying to catch a moonbeam in a bottle. Something was always missing. I didn't realize it then but it was that personal relationship with Jesus Christ that I desperately needed. It was His peace that I wanted but didn't have.

GOD PROTECTED ME

For a short time, while I was single again, I started running with a motorcycle gang, and saw a lot of my friends either arrested, badly injured, or killed. The lifestyle was loaded with drugs and other abuses.

Strangely though, I still sensed the providential hand of God on my life. Because of that, the Devil and his seducing music, drugs, and sex didn't have me wrapped tightly enough to take complete control of me. But I was getting tired of the lifestyle, so I kind of remained on the fringes and didn't get in too deep. Even though some folks may have called me a heathen, I continued to feel that I could walk away whenever I wanted to.

THE SATISFIER

Let me ask you this: Are you in that place right now? Have you been seeking but not finding? Unless you really meet Jesus, you probably won't even know what you're looking for. But once you find Him, it will all become so clear; you'll wonder how you ever missed Him for so long.

You can try everything on the planet, but only Jesus is *the Satisfier!* Only He can fill your emptiness and calm you at every twist and turn in the road. Only He can satisfy your wanderings and bring true peace into your life.

God has much to offer that will help you find fullness for today, faith for tomorrow, and hope for eternity. But you must decide to walk with Him instead of the world in order to reap His blessings.

Dancing with the world and the Devil will never bring you into God's care. He cannot and will not walk in your filth and mire just so you can have your way. You do have the freedom to run wherever you want to, but not in His presence, and not under His protection. Without God's covering, Satan can have a field day with you. You'll become a slave to the world, the flesh, and the Devil and you'll never win against those odds in your own strength.

CHAPTER SIX

A BLAST FROM THE PAST

I spent 1963 gallivanting around the countryside. I needed to fill the terrible void I had after breaking up with Judy and losing my three kids to her. Then, in the Spring of '64, I met a beautiful, intelligent young lady by the name of Janni. I seriously would like to have settled down with her for a long while; maybe even marry again. Things were looking up, I thought. But then, I got an awful blast from the past.

Within a few short months of knowing Janni, I had a phone call telling me that Judy had abandoned two of our children. At only four years old, and nine months old, they were alone for four days and four nights. The situation finally surfaced when my four-year-old, Doug Jr., could no longer find food to eat, nor could he change the diaper for his nine-month-old sister. So he wandered off in search of help. To this day, I'm amazed at how God took care of them.

"Dougie" walked across a busy boulevard to a woman he saw, to ask for help. She was out in her yard raking leaves when he approached her. You would never guess in a million years who this woman was. She was the same person that had gone to high school with my older sister!

Well, when the woman learned who this little boy was, she called my sister, Neva, who in turn called me, in Dallas, Texas, and told me what happened. I immediately flew to Illinois to get my children.

I was in absolute shock! I never thought Judy would abandon our kids that way! And I never dreamed of what I would find out next: my daughter, Dawn, who was only two years old, was missing!

31

There I was, joyfully holding my four-year-old son and my nine-month-old daughter, and at the same time, I was suffering indescribable heartache because Dawn was nowhere to be found.

Neva, my sister, decided to call Judy's mom to see if she knew anything about the disappearance. That's when we learned what had happened. Here's the rest of the story:

After Judy and I separated for the last time, she went to live in Beloit, Wisconsin with her mother. While her mom and grandparents were in California on vacation, Judy did the most unconscionable, unspeakable, unforgivable thing a parent can do, next to murder. She gave away our middle daughter, Dawn Marie. Well, actually, she didn't just give her away, she *sold* her for ten thousand dollars! That's right, $10,000.00; the going price for a child on the black market in Chicago.

The mother of my children sold my daughter through an illegal adoption process and took the money and ran.

It was told to me in this way: Judy was walking down the street when a couple passed her on the sidewalk, only to turn back and stop her for a moment saying, "My, what a pretty little girl you have. I sure wish we could have children, but we can't"

And Judy's response was, "Oh, you think she's cute, do you? Would you like to have her?"

And that's how the illegal adoption began. From there, they later made the trip to Chicago where everything was finalized and my daughter was given over.

I was so grateful to have recovered two of my children, but I was still so depressed and worried over Dawn as I returned home to Dallas. My heart was aching and I had so many questions.

Thankfully, my new girlfriend, Janni, helped and supported me emotionally through the entire ordeal. Because of that, I decided to ask her to move in with me to help me take care of my children. We also began the long and arduous search for my missing daughter. That was no way to start a family, but it's what we found ourselves trying to do as I committed myself a second time aboard the "marriage-merry-go-round".

WEDDING BELLS AGAIN

I think Janni and I met in June or July of 1964, and we both knew we wanted to be together. So we lived together as man and wife, raising the kids. We were like a true family and didn't feel convicted about our common-law lifestyle. We didn't think much about living outside God's sanctioned marriage boundaries; at least I wasn't.

I had tried legal marriage with the license and the preacher and all the trimmings which were supposed to assure me of lifelong happiness but it didn't seem to work. So, now it wasn't a priority for me. I just wanted to be loved and to give love back. As long as I had that, the paper-work didn't matter. The free-love idea of the wild early 60s was good enough for me, but even though we had the appearance of marriage and family, still there was something missing.

It's dangerous for folks to just live together without real commitments. Marriage forms a bond that can fight off the world when it comes at you, but simply living together lacks the strength of that tie. It's just not the same. Marriage vows are important.

It was another poor choice on my part, but I continued in the relationship. I guess God was letting me *run my course*. Why? Perhaps so this thick-headed, know-it-all, (*me*), could learn a valuable, shareable lesson.

Janni and I had great dreams for the future in spite of our very 60s lifestyle. We even had a child together. She was a beautiful baby girl, born on April 18th, 1966. We named her Cynthia Lynn.

Destiny, however, would have it that she would die seven weeks later. It was June 6th, 1966. Cynthia Lynn Veer was overtaken by what is known as SIDS, (sudden infant death syndrome). As for Janni and me, that spelled the beginning of the end.

A couple of years after Cindy died we had another child, a son, who we named Kirk. He was born July 2, 1970. Following his birth, we finally got married. The special day was September 14th, 1970.

STREET GOSPEL

Janni and I moved back to Dallas, Texas, after the wedding, to try to make a go of things. But we never managed to recover from the loss of our daughter. Because our marriage wasn't holding up at all, I tried to get away from it by diving headfirst into the entertainment world. I hooked up with an acid rock band. Strangely enough, it was called "Street Gospel", but it had nothing to do with the Gospel of Jesus Christ.

Anyway, we hit the road, playing in New Orleans, Dallas, and Birmingham. And with that, all of the old temptations for drugs returned. Now I was using and selling, but for some reason, I guess God continued to look after me, protecting me from deep addiction, legal problems, avoiding arrest, and even death.

For a guy who was only in his late twenties, I had been through an awful lot already. I had faced death in a submarine and came close to it again as a biker. My daughter had been sold and illegally adopted out, and I didn't know if I'd ever find her again. Then another daughter died. I had one marriage go bad, and I was now facing my second divorce. I felt like I was literally losing my mind.

I wanted to know God but I was living outside of His will. God, in turn, cannot and will not bless sin. Period. It's that simple. I was in it up to my neck, so I had no right to expect anything but pain and sorrow in my life.

The Bible says, ***"Be not deceived; God is not mocked: for whatsoever a man sows, that shall he also reap,"*** (Galatians 6:7; KJV).

I knew better but I was still hard-headed enough to continue doing things my own way. I guess God was allowing me a lot of leeway but I was paying an extremely high price for that kind of freedom. All in all, I never dreamed life could get any worse . . . but it did.

CHAPTER SEVEN

MISS LUCY

As of 1969, Janni and I had lived together for four and a half years. Regardless of what was or wasn't working, I'm sure--unbeknown to us--God was quietly working on our behalf, keeping our best interests at heart.

God has an important plan for each of our lives and it's a perfect plan; one that He has crafted just for each of us. We can walk in that plan but we need to stop running long enough to let Him reveal it.

The Bible says, **"God is not willing that any should perish,"** (II Peter 3:9; KJV). Receiving eternal life is the first step in God's plan. He longs for us to come to Him and He is always trying to draw us.

Janni and I were definitely lost and God was trying to draw both of us. I know that's why we found ourselves living next door to a very saintly woman who would not let go of me. She was like a bulldog with a bone! Yes, her name was Lucille Lancaster of Dallas, Texas, and knowing that dear lady was definitely God's plan!

The story really takes place in Highland, Texas, a small community land-locked inside of the boundaries of Dallas. It was like an island, sitting quietly in the middle of a metropolis of busy freeways and wild city living. It was a peaceful little oasis with its own quiet little lifestyle.

YOUNG AT HEART

We lived in the Cloister Apartments. Next door to our apartment building was a house where this elderly lady lived, whom I came to know as Miss Lucy.

Miss Lucy was born in that house some 80 years earlier. She was a member of Highland Baptist Church, where her mother and father had been members. Miss Lucy's house was completely hemmed in by a chain link fence. Most people her age have a hard time walking, but she used to run the perimeter of her yard with her little dog.

Miss Lucy also drove a full-sized automobile--an Oldsmobile--that was as big as a boat, but you should have seen her drive that thing! She would back it out of the driveway, put it in gear, and *swoosh,* down the street she went like a teenager. Sometimes, she'd even squeal the tires. None of the teenagers had anything on Miss Lucy.

I'm not saying she was a *wild* woman. She was anything but that. She was sharp, alert, active, and in control. In short, Miss Lucy wasn't one of your run-of-the-mill little old ladies. She was blessed with vitality and youthfulness.

I think God kept Miss Lucy young at heart because she was pleasing to Him. Agility and ability in the golden years of life are often benefits of the Christian life. Lucy was always telling people about the Lord, so God allowed her to keep on keeping on. She was a blessing to many people, and as it turns out, a very special blessing to me.

CHRISTIAN LOVE

Miss Lucy used to come over to our apartment on Saturdays to talk to me about Jesus and invite us to church. (Janni never seemed to be around during those visits.) I don't know how Miss Lucy always managed to catch up with me, but I guess she must have watched for me to come home. Then as soon as I did, she'd be knocking at my front door. I'd let her in and she'd sit next to me on the couch, patting my knee, inviting me to church, and just *smiling all over the place!*

Picture it, here she was, and here I was. I had been in a bike gang, I had worked big construction jobs with lots of guys, I had been in the Navy, and I had lived on the streets in several big cities, and boy, did I have a bad, bad mouth. Yet here she was, a gracious old saint, pure as pure can be, and she was seeking my company. It must have been God's love that made her do it. Nothing else made sense.

Well, I made up my mind that I didn't like this woman. I didn't like her telling me I could change for the better if I would just come to church and accept Jesus. I thought, "Man, alive. I'm not stupid! I know about Jesus. I've known about Him ever since I was a child in Sunday school. Of course, I'm gonna get to go to Heaven. I haven't killed anyone and I'm not a heathen because . . . well . . . because I'm an American! Besides, I've been to church before. What's wrong with this lady? And just exactly what's wrong with my life, anyway?"

(In my quiet hours alone; however, the question haunted me: "What *was* wrong with my life?" I didn't have an answer.)

Although I knew she was a nice lady, I began to dread her visits. They made me uncomfortable. She was always kind and she never told me how bad I was, or that I was destined for Hell because of my lifestyle. Instead, she spoke lovingly with a big, beautiful smile. And she told me what Jesus could do for me, that He was good, that He loved me, and that my life would be so much better if I'd let Him into my heart. She never told me what was wrong with me. She just loved me!

Even so, I didn't like her always coming over. I especially didn't like those wrinkled old hands and the way she would pat my knee with them all the time. To me, those creases in her hands represented death, and that scared me to pieces! I didn't want to look at death, or even think about it. I needed to show her once and for all, that I just wasn't interested in what she was peddling and that she needed to get off my back!

CATCH ME IF YOU CAN

Yes, I needed to out-smart Miss Lucy. I needed to figure out a way to get rid of her. I thought if I lied and promised her I'd come to church, and then not show up, she'd leave me alone. Yeah, that sounded like a good plan to me, so I tried it. Did she give up? No.

My next idea was to just stay away from home more, and come in at different times when she'd be too tired to watch for me. But that didn't work either. She was always at my door, and so I'd let her in.

Then I decided that if I would pour out my bad language on her, and if it was bad enough, maybe she'd leave me alone. But she didn't stay away no matter what I said. She was impossible!

Then I decided to take things one step further. I came up with the idea that I would actually go to church with her, and I'd take my bad manners and foul language with me. That was it! I thought if I embarrassed her enough she would absolutely never invite me to church again. Now I just had to set the plan in motion. Hey, was I smart or what? As a matter of fact, I was a genius! I could hardly wait to get started.

CHAPTER EIGHT

MY FIRST VISIT TO CHURCH

As usual, that Saturday afternoon she was at my door inviting me to church the next day. I accepted. To my disappointment, she wasn't even surprised. Sunday morning came, and I found myself standing beside her in the sanctuary as she proudly introduced me to everyone like I was her own son. I didn't know what to say. I did absolutely nothing to carry out my nasty plan. As the old expression goes: I came, I saw, I went back into the house. But I hoped my going with her would at least get her off my back.

Another week went by, and then Saturday came. And there she was at my door again. I really wanted her to go away, so I didn't answer. She came back the very next afternoon, on Sunday! I could see I wasn't going to be rid of her easily so I opened the door and she said, "Hi Doug-o-las. How did you like the service last Sunday?"

I muttered a raspy, disinterested, "I dunno . . ."

"Well Doug-o-las" she said, turning my name into a three syllable word, "Would you come to church with me this evening?"

"No, Miss Lucille, I won't. Really, I'd rather not go tonight, O.K.?" She quietly and graciously accepted my answer and left.

When Saturday came around again, she invited me again. But again, I said no. A third Saturday came and went, but the answer was still no. She continued, however, to show up for her regular Saturday visits, which for her must have been like a long, hard term on the mission field.

It was now four weeks since I went to church with Miss Lucy, but she continued coming over faithfully, asking and inviting me to church. I would only whine, "Miss Lucy, I already went with you once. That ought-ta be enough." But she had an uncanny way of pouring out her love while reeling me in with her snappy answers.

She said, "Doug-o-las? Do you know what tomorrow is?"

I answered, "No." And I didn't care, either.

"Tomorrow is Easter. Don't you think everyone should go to church at Easter, Christmas, and Thanksgiving?"

"Well . . ." I stuttered, "I don't think people go to church at Thanksgiving . . . just Easter and Christmas. Besides, Thanksgiving is always on a Thursday."

Miss Lucy said, "But they do go on Easter, right?"

I said, "Yeah, I guess so."

"Good." she said, "Then I'll see you in the morning about 10:30!" With that, she turned on her heel and was out the door before I could say a word. I stood there with my jaw hanging and thought, "What in the world have I gotten myself into? Did I just agree to go with her? I guess so, but that means I'm gonna have to go to church again. Doggies! Am I stupid or what? Mmm . . . maybe *this* will be my chance to really mess things up. I'll just cuss, and act bad, and embarrass her like I wanted to the last time. Maybe then she'll finally give up on me."

MY SECOND VISIT TO CHURCH

Would you like to guess what happened on my second visit to church? Nothing. Nada. Zip. Zero. I didn't say a blasted word. I had missed another opportunity and wondered what I would do next. She

41

would still be after me. And before I knew it, there she was back at my door that very afternoon.

Lucille Lancaster reminds me of the woman found in Luke 18:1-5. The story in this passage is about a woman who kept going to a judge, asking for his help. Although he kept refusing her, she persisted until he got so tired of her that he finally gave in to her wishes. Maybe that's what made Miss Lucy the woman she was. I've often wondered if perhaps she modeled herself after that New Testament saint.

In any case, Lucille definitely had been led by the Holy Spirit in putting up with the likes of me. I already decided I had *had it* with her. She had bugged me all I could stand, and the next time she showed up I was really going to let her have it. In my own, rough language I planned to tell her not to *ever* bother me again! But then she changed the game.

After going to church with her Easter morning, Miss Lucy came back again that Sunday afternoon. The knock at the door woke me from my sleep and put me in a bad mood. Yes, there she was: Miss Lucy "do good".

I was positive I would make this the end of her visits. I fully intended to refuse her and let her know I was really through.

"Doug-o-las, wasn't that a nice service this morning?" she asked with that long, suffering smile of hers.

"Yeah, yeah," I mumbled. "I guess so.".

"Won't you come back tonight? It's really going to be special."

"Miss Lucy, I'm not going back with you. I'm through. I'm done. I've gone with you *twice*, so now *leave me alone!*" My voice had raised into a loud pitch.

In that seemingly eternal moment, the air captured the echo of my words. Then there was silence. They say silence is golden but at that moment, it was eery and dark. The smile that had once lighted the whole room was gone. The kind, sweetness that had beamed from her eyes had turned into an icy, piercing gaze. Miss Lucy looked me dead in the eye and deep into my soul. I knew there was something very serious in what she was about to say.

She spoke softly, "Doug-o-las. I promise you, if you'll come to church tonight, I'll *never* bother you again." Her words hung in the air, waiting for an answer.

I wondered what to say but I wasn't sure. I should have been happy; ecstatic even, that she had just promised to leave me alone. But I wasn't glad and I couldn't figure out why.

A chill came over me and I heard myself say, "O.K. I'll go, but you'd better keep your word and stop bothering me after this." Her eyes burned deep into mine, and that in itself was her answer to me.

MY THIRD VISIT TO CHURCH
The Pastor's name was Harold Freeman but I don't remember what he preached. I do remember he was bald from the front to the middle of his head. He was missing a lot of hair for his young age and standing there in the pulpit, he had a certain glow about him. It was like the lights from Heaven were shining down on him, not the lights from the church ceiling. Whatever it was, he looked especially *clean*.

As for me, I was so completely surrounded by the love of Christ that even if the preacher's sermon had been "Mary had a little lamb," God would have moved upon my heart that evening, and that's just what He did.

I remember standing up when the invitation was given. I must have somehow floated down to the altar because honestly, I can't remember walking to it. Suddenly, I was just there!

At that moment I knew fully that Jesus had died for me, and had risen again, and was in Heaven, waiting to help me. I also knew that my life was full of all kinds of sin and I was unworthy of God's love, yet He was the only one who could forgive me. With unashamed tears of brokenness and joy, I accepted Jesus Christ as my Savior and Lord. I will never forget what Christ did for me that night.

I was kneeling at the altar, crying out to God, when out of nowhere someone from behind me placed their hands on my shoulders, and I felt comforted. I crossed my arms in front of me and reached back for those hands, only to discover they belonged to Miss Lucy. I held on tightly to those dear, old, wrinkled hands; the hands I once so despised. Then, in the middle of it all, Lucille's sweet voice whispered into my ear, "Doug-o-las, don't you know you need Jesus?"

That did it. The flood gates of my soul opened and my eyes filled up and spilled over with the love of Christ. He filled me to overflowing, making me feel cleaner than I had felt in a long, long time. There in that place I didn't want to be, on that wonderful Easter Sunday evening, I could finally declare, "I'm His, I'm His. Thank you, Jesus. Thank you for the cross. Thank you for dying in my place. Thank you for loving me and making me whole."

CHAPTER NINE

BORN-AGAIN, BUT UNCHANGED

I'd *like* to tell you that after becoming a born-again Christian, I went on to victory and served the Lord faithfully. That would be a wonderful place to end this story, but the truth is, I didn't know what I was supposed to do. I didn't understand how to walk the walk, and I surely didn't know how to talk the talk.

I had accepted forgiveness for my sins, but I hadn't yet learned that I needed God's power. Only He could keep sin's rule from ruining my life. I went from being a lost sinner to a saved sinner. I had moved up to the next level: "carnal" Christianity. But this was not what God had intended for me.

Instead of pursuing God, I took to roaming the winding, twisting roads of the world, caught in all of its spidery webs of wine, women, and song. I was confused and frustrated. I wanted to live the way I saw other Christians living, but I wasn't measuring up; I was a baby in Christ and I stayed that way for some time. I was torn between right living and living a life of sin, which was the only lifestyle I had known up until then.

My marital life was shamefully filled with lust and irresponsible failures as well. I say lust because I experienced a form of love that was merely sensual. I had not yet learned about the agapé kind of love so necessary for a long-lasting relationship.

At the time of my conversion, Janni and I had only been married for 18 months, although we had lived together before that for a few years. Being that I was a new Christian, I tried to share Jesus with her, but it caused a wedge to grow between us that grew larger every day. I didn't know what to do about it. Finally, she decided to take off with some truck driver taking our son with her. That led to our divorce and my world was upside down *again*. I, in turn, took my son and daughter by my previous wife, Judy, and also left.

OLD WAYS

I drove a thousand miles north to Wisconsin and dropped my children off with their maternal grandmother. I desperately needed to find out what was going on in my head and why I had failed to live like I was supposed to. I should have asked God to help me, but instead, I found myself looking for a rum bottle and a woman.

When I was around men I was hard and coarse. But I was always kind and gentle to women, so girlfriends were easy to find. Besides that, I was handsome, and pleasant to be with; I had the gift of gab and girls liked that. I could really pour on the flattery, too. (I later learned that flattery is merely a form of lying!) I was always trying to fill the void in my life with sensuality, and the devil always had a lady in the wings to entice me.

The wild "if it feels good do it" movement of the 60s had spilled over into the 70s and I found myself still identifying with that. So I dated various women: I met a girl who was a ballet dancer, then one who was a model, and another one who had a millionaire father, but none of them worked out.

In 1971 or so, I met another beautiful girl, Terri. She was gorgeous, fun to be with, and married, but that wasn't going well for her. I didn't want to, but I tore myself away from that situation and went back to Texas. Within a couple of days, she flew to Dallas and met me there. We reunited and drove to Colorado to meet her family; they were wonderful people. Following that, we lived together for a while in Louisiana, and I fell deeply in love with her, but sadly, it came to an end. I just couldn't seem to get my feet on the ground and establish any kind of a solid, worthwhile life.

Overall, people liked me and accepted me as a good person, but inwardly, my lifestyle was far from the new life God expected me to live. So, I just bounced around the countryside, city to city, state to state, which was bad for me, and unhealthy for my two children whom I was supposed to be responsible for. I knew there was more to the Christian life than this but I was missing it, and I couldn't figure out how to find it.

GOD'S LOVE

The free-love-Jesus-movement was winding down. I had been sucked into all that "flower-power" stuff but I was getting very tired of it. I was saved but I still wasn't very spiritual. I could talk the talk now but I wasn't walking the walk. And I remained confused over the difference between "love" and "sensuality." I still thought they were the same thing.

Somewhere along the way, I met a girl named Lisa. Lisa was a good person, though, at times, I didn't want to be around her. We would live together for a while. Then I'd get ticked off at her, pack my stuff, and move out. Somehow she always managed to find me, and we'd start all over, living together in sin.

Again, I'd disappear, only to meet up with her later on down the road. This went on for two years! It was unfair to her, unfair to me, and definitely unfair to my kids. I failed to give them any kind of stability or a proper example of a solid marriage and a good home life. Worse than that, I knew I was breaking the heart of God.

It's amazing that He put up with me during all of that, sparing me of any serious chastisement. The Bible says God is patient, long-suffering, and full of tender mercies. I found that to be true. Here I was, a professing Christian, yet I was uncommitted to Jesus Christ. I was earthly and sensual, and I was getting by with it, or so it seemed.

I was still letting the Devil call the shots. He would play his "fiddle of fantasies" and I would dance to the music. It's unreal to see how low a man can sink when he has nothing but worldly pleasures to live for. He doesn't care about doing anything good for himself or others. He just lives for momentary indulgences.

Of course, God never really lets us get by with sin because He knows too well about the hurt it causes. He allowed me to go just so far and then He'd put something in my way to change my course. Yes, He loved me as His child, even though I continually hurt Him. In spite of my rebellion, He continued to work out his plan for my life.

So, for the time being, God let me go on in my own ways, stumbling and falling down while remaining faithfully by my side to pick up the broken pieces. He was continually watching over me. I was His new baby; His weak child whom He loved with an everlasting, unconditional love. I needed a lot of support and God gave me just that. He kept His word to never leave or forsake me no matter how much I failed.

Think about it: how much do you love your children? How much do you put up with their mistakes? As much as we love our children, our heavenly Father loves us more. He is the Creator, the Author, and the Finisher of love. For the sake of agapé love, He bought and paid for our sins through the giving of His only Son, Jesus.

Looking back, I realize how much God suffered through my rebellious years. He didn't throw me away. His love for me was a constant even during my very worst times. I didn't understand it then, but now that I have grown children I do. Now I can better grasp the depth and the breadth of God's love. I see how immeasurable it is and I haven't even begun to scratch the surface. I know one thing for sure: God loved me.

CHAPTER TEN

THE SECOND LAST WALTZ

I wanted to get my life straightened out so God wouldn't have to put up with my unruliness anymore. I wanted to quit being disobedient and I wanted to please the Lord in everything. Lisa was in and out of my life a dozen times or more but I was determined to let her go. Then I would be free to live the righteous Christian life I so desired.

The Devil fought me every step of the way, however. He tried to convince me I was still the same miserable hypocrite as before, and with that being said, he continued to control me. How you ask? One word, Lisa. He did it through the sensual sway of a woman. That was the final frontier for me.

It was late one night, about 2:00 am when I woke up to find Lisa sitting on the edge of my bed, staring at me. Somehow she found me and was ready to play house again. I have to admit she was always seductively tempting. She was also young and impressionable, and I guess she loved me very much, and I was weak. Taking her back was more my fault than hers. As she sat there, speaking to me in those soft tones, I toyed with the idea that our relationship could work after all.

I thought maybe, if I gave myself to her properly, and settled down, maybe . . . it could work. I wanted to make it happen; I wanted to dance this waltz again. But I was at a loss as to how to bring it about, so I *played* her. I simply told her what she wanted to hear and I'm very, very sorry about that. Looking back, I have to say Lisa was a good person and she deserved better than me.

So why couldn't I get it together? I guess I was always drawn to the exciting aspects of life which gave me nothing foundational to build on. I ended up in the wrong places and hung around with the wrong people, even the wrong so-called *church* people. Some of them weren't much help at all.

Lisa and I were turbulent together. It was the same old story, over and over again. I was supposed to be a new creature in Christ, a living example to my children, and even to her. But I never gave Jesus one *inch* of my will. I did everything in my own strength; it was a losing battle. Case in point: whenever Lisa came back, including this time, it was like all my resolve went out the window.

THE MUSIC PLAYED ON

Loneliness is like a taskmaster. It can make a person weak, no matter how much one tries to be strong and live right. Because of my weakness, real change never had a chance to take root in my new heart. And I didn't want to talk about it or even face it, like so many other new, back-slid Christians. Like them, I just wanted to go on, living in denial.

In our humanness, we never want to admit our failures and spiritual weaknesses. Some Christians are legalistic and pious. They are so "holier than thou" and so "heavenly minded" that they are no earthly good. I was on the flip side of that coin. I had become so earthly minded, I was no heavenly good. I thought I could have my cake and eat it too; live as I pleased and still please God.

At the same time, I thought I could let a few Christian sounding phrases pop out of my mouth, go to church once in a while, and get by. But God was saying, "You can't do that, and please Me too."

Unfortunately, I wasn't listening. Instead, I tuned in to the hypnotizing sounds of Satan's fiddle. He played all the right tunes to satisfy my sensual man. Every melody drew me to my fleshly will instead of the Lord's godly strength.

So I took Lisa back one more time and the roller-coaster went around one more time. What a weak person I was, but thankfully, God understood.

GOD AND HYPOCRITES

When I lay my head down on the pillow at night, I knew before the Lord that I was a sorry human being. And I was ready to be done. Have you ever been there? Do you know what I'm trying to say? It's an awful place to be, isn't it? If you really belong to God, then the fleshly, make believe, religious life is not enjoyable. Trying to keep one foot in the sin-life and one foot in God's will is no fun.

I was a miserable child, caught between a rock and a hard place. My Christian friends didn't want to be with me because I was so shallow. And my non-Christian friends didn't like me either. I had God stamped all over me even though I was a back-slider. I would only go so far into their lifestyles, and no more.

So I became like a worthless, old wet shoe, thrown out along the roadside; no good to anyone. I would either have to kick God out of my life and face eternity without Him or else get serious. Thankfully, God pulled me out of that mucky, slimy life and cleaned me up so I could get back on track with Him.

I TRADED MY PRIZED POSSESSION

I had a 1965 Ford-500 convertible that I discovered in the back row of a car lot. (I told you I like convertibles, remember?) But it was in such deplorable condition when I found it, that it actually had grass growing through the scantily carpeted floorboards. Imagination might tell you how dirty the rest of the car was after having sat there for several years.

At the same time, the body was straight and solid. And when I put the jumper cables to it, it turned over a couple of times and fired right up! It ran just as smooth as anything I had ever owned. It truly was love at first sight.

In between driving it, it took me two years to rebuild it. I put that car back into near perfect condition. I added a few coats of British racing green and a thin gold pinstripe. I installed a very dark, red leather interior. I gave it a new white convertible top, and I added gold wheels with baby-moon chrome center caps.

Then I put wide slicks on the back and tuned it up so it was in perfect, dependable, operating condition. It really was my pride and joy! I traveled many enjoyable miles in it and there was nothing you could have done to talk me out of that car! Well, almost nothing.

You see, Lisa was still an on-again-off-again problem. No matter how secretly I'd disappear, she'd always find me. I genuinely wanted to be free of her; I was tired of living a defeated Christian life. I just had to break away, so I did the unthinkable: I gave Lisa my baby. No, not a real baby. My amazing '65 Ford convertible!

Yup. I handed over the title and the whole nine yards, and said, "Go back up North to your home and family and don't ever come to see me again. Find a life, better than the one I've given you. Please . . . just go."

I made a choice. I gave up my prized possession so that I wouldn't waltz with sin any longer. Not that it was her fault! I don't want this to sound like I was blaming her. Even though she was young and innocent, I was easily tempted.

I just came to the place where I had to stop doing the same old things the same old way. I wanted more of Christ in my life and I wanted to quit disappointing Him. I learned right then, that if you really mean business with God, He will really do business with you. He will give you everything you need to be whole and complete and accomplish things far beyond your wildest dreams.

So I guess I traded in my car for peace with the Lord. Lisa knew exactly why I did it, too. She saw that I wanted to make a brand new commitment to Jesus and that I was very serious this time. She accepted my terms and kept her word, thus ending our relationship. I've always been thankful to her for that.

CHAPTER ELEVEN

DO I HEAR BELLS AGAIN?

The weeks and months passed and I became interested in a woman named Nora, who lived next door to me. We met in June of 1974, and by September we were walking down the aisle. Imagine that!

I'll never forget our wedding day because I was wearing a body brace under my tuxedo. She and I stood there with my young son and daughter, as I suffered in pain from a broken collar bone and a separated shoulder. I had been in a recent motorcycle wreck. Yes, hiding behind that "newlywed smile" was a man who was really hurting.

There was something else bothering me too, though. A still, small voice inside my head kept saying, "Don't do it, Doug. Don't marry her. Stop now. You have to get out while you can. Don't worry about how it will look. Just stop and get away!"

Was that God talking to me? I don't know. Of course, I thought maybe the pain killers were working a number on my head, so I ignored the warning, and let the day run its course.

It was September 14th, 1974. Nora had been working at an auto dealership in Birmingham, Alabama, during the day, and at a bar in the evenings. She quit both jobs to start her future with me.

I was doing custom graphics, air-brushing scenery onto bikes, vans, cars, trucks, and dune buggies. Then, I got a contract to custom build an A-frame home in Talladega, so we moved there so I could complete the job and get back into construction.

Soon, my bride and I were launching into our brand new life believing things would be changing for us. I still clearly remember that moving day. The four of us excitedly packed our belongings as we got ready to go to our new place. It was late and we were tired but anxious to head out, so we traveled to Talladega by dark. As we drove along, one thought kept going through my mind: "This is the last time I'm going to move!" I didn't want to be bouncing all over the country anymore. I wanted stability.

HAPPILY EVER AFTER

As we settled in Talladega, our lives blossomed with all the joys of stable family life. Nora was a very good wife who loved me and loved the kids. In fact, she was better for them than their real mother was.

I'll always remember the start of each school year. Nora would take the kids shopping for clothes and for all the other necessities. (That used to be my job.) I was blessed to have a partner in life who would step in and take care of the many things a real Mom was supposed to do. The longer we were together, the more I grew to love her.

I took pride in my wife, but I regret that I didn't tell her often enough. I had become so busy with work that I was thoughtless and uncaring at times. If I were to shoulder any fault or blame, that's what I would say.

My hours were filled as a job foreman for the Daniels Construction Company, an international, commercial building company. At the time, we were adding a large addition onto the Kimberly-Clark plant in Childersburg, Alabama. The pay was great, but the 10 hour work day, and the 40-mile drive back and forth took up all my time.

In spite of our challenges, I thought Nora and I worked really well together as a family. Those were good times, and we prospered in many ways. I was happy once again being a husband and a father. I was thrilled when we bought our first home, and even more thrilled when our first child was born: a little baby girl we named Jaimée.

JAIMÉE

A few years before I met Nora, she had had an abortion. Later, she became pregnant again and gave birth to a son whom she gave to her husband's parents in Louisiana when he was just a few months old. After all that, Nora thought God was a big monster in the sky and was looking down on her to punish her by not allowing her to have another baby. Jaimée was exactly what Nora needed to restore her self-esteem and realize that God wasn't going to punish her for her past sins.

Jaimée came to us on February 13th, 1976, just hours before Valentine's Day. We always called her our Valentine baby. Her arrival was a wonderful gift which became a bonding factor for our new family. It's like she was teaching us a new way to love.

Even at 18 months, she was outgoing toward everyone, wherever we went and was always willing to give a happy smile and a hug. She became the brightest spot in our entire family. I swear the whole world got its first ray of sunshine from her each morning when she awoke.

One of her greatest joys was to see pictures of Jesus. She always insisted on being held up to touch his bearded face. Then she would say, "Zeesus," with that sweet and tender, childish voice. I had a beard, too, but we were convinced that had absolutely nothing to do with it. She was genuinely attracted to the Lord.

DAD RONSON

Soon after our move, we also wanted to establish our church life. We were disappointed though because the churches we visited weren't what we thought they should be. So we quit going for a while, and I spent many Sundays riding around on my motorcycle. Of course, that affected my whole family and we just sort of drifted away from church attendance.

Then we met Pastor Harold Ronson and his wife. They adopted us, so-to-speak, and took us under their wings like we were family. They became Mom and Dad to us. What made our bonding stronger than ever was the fact that I had no living Father, and Nora had no living Mother.

Nora started attending Mrs. Ronson's weekly home Bible study next door, and I began attending a one-on-one discipleship class on Saturday mornings with Pastor Ronson. Through that, we eventually got back into a real, productive, church life.

The Ronsons became more than just the Pastor and his wife. They were our spiritual mentors and friends. Dad was the only man that ever cared to counsel me spiritually. I guess that's because his whole life was tied up in Christ and he really lived that love-your-neighbor thing. He had only one rule: "Put Jesus first!" He not only said it over and over, but he practiced it every day of his life.

I knew this was the beginning of something new. It was a spiritual awakening; an honest relationship with God. I knew the time for my play-acting was over. Whatever lay ahead for me was going to be serious and worthwhile. Dad Ronson came into my life just when I really needed a man of wisdom to turn to. He was the only true advisor/mentor I ever had.

CHAPTER TWELVE

WHY BIBLE COLLEGE?

I decided to get into a new line of work. I became a Confidential Informant, (CI), and I worked with the Drug Enforcement Administration, (DEA) because of my past history with drugs and dealers. It was a good fit.

My job was to buy drugs and gather information that I would pass along through the proper channels, hopefully, to gain arrests and convictions.

I was doing well until one night in an abandoned, run-down crack-house, I saw what looked like some rags wrapped around the back of an unbelievably filthy commode. Thinking there may be a stash of drugs there, I reached down to pull out the rags. That's when I realized I was tugging on the body of a young girl. There was hardly a spot on her naked flesh that wasn't black, blue, green, or purple. She may have weighed 50 pounds or less, and she was dead. Someone had taken all that this 12-year-old had to give. And once she became addicted and worthless to them, they dumped her there to die.

I sat down and cried before God. "There's something wrong with what I'm doing. What is it? Here I am, trying my best to carry out a good public service. I'm getting drugs off the streets and I'm getting drug dealers busted. And this is what I find! Why? Am I not doing enough to help?"

As I poured my heart out to the Lord, I realized I should be reaching these kids *before* they get to this point in their lives. Simply busting these suppliers did not help save them. By then, it was too late. I had to reach these young people *before* they destroyed themselves.

That experience drew me, in part, to a decision I made only a couple of weeks later to attend Toccoa Falls Bible College. I wanted to get the training I needed to reach these lost and dying young folks. With God's life-changing words, many lives could be kept from ending like that of the girl I found in the bathroom that night.

PUTTING JESUS FIRST

The next evening, after finding that poor little soul, I got into it with a "Gold-Shield" agent who was making money on the side, trying to work both sides of the fence. Earlier that week, I also had a run-in with another agent and a brush with death. Yeah, I got really mad during an argument with him which then turned physical. I took his gold shield and threw it across the fence into the high-school football field. I'm glad the fight ended there.

I thought about it the next day and went to find the badge so I could return it to the guy. But once I retrieved it, I changed my mind. The shield never went back to him after all, because I figured he didn't deserve it. I did have a brother-in-law who was a Deputy Sheriff. In my eyes, he did deserve it so I gave the gold shield to him.

For me, this was the last stop on the train. There wasn't going to be any more running and roaming, even if I thought it was for a good cause. I had to put my roots down and start making a truly respectable life for my wife and my kids. I was closer to God now, but I'm sure He was getting tired of my poor, failing ideas, as was I.

I had no concrete plans for the future, but I had a strong yearning to return to my first love: Jesus. I wanted to dance with Him, and Him alone. My last waltz with the Devil had finally reached its end. It was time--as Dad Ronson would have so sensibly said--to "put Jesus first".

CALLED TO THE MINISTRY

My walk with the Lord really grew in Talladega. To be honest, I have to thank the Ronsons for it. They steered me faithfully toward Jesus Christ, so much so, that I became open and committed to God's call on my life.

God impressed upon me that I should go into the ministry, possibly full time. A brand new thing was being birthed in my spirit; that is, in my spiritual man. God's hand was resting on me. He wanted to guide my life in a new direction.

One afternoon, sitting together in my living room and talking, Dad Ronson listened intently to me as I told him I felt I should become a minister. After a time, he leaned forward and pointed his index finger at me and made the most amazing statement. It was something I did not expect to hear. He said, "Doug, don't ever, ever go into the ministry."

I stared at him in disbelief and stuttered "But . . . but . . . you . . . ." You see, he had been in ministry about six decades!

He continued, "Don't interrupt me." I didn't know what to think but when he spoke again it made sense.

"Doug, don't ever, ever go into the ministry . . . " He paused again and silence filled the room. I could hear my heart beating.

". . . that is . . . unless God closes every other door of opportunity, and you are positive that you're *called of God*. Many people are sent into the ministry but few are called."

It was a heart to heart discussion and through it, I found peace with God as to my calling. Dad and I agreed that Bible college was to be the next step in my journey. So I began to make plans accordingly. I thank God for the wisdom and encouragement Dad poured into me.

A PLACE CALLED BEAUTIFUL

The Fall of 1977 was drawing near when I realized we would be moving again. The place? Toccoa Falls College, (TFC), in Toccoa, Georgia. It was a beautiful place, nestled in the foothills of the Blue Ridge mountains.

We already had some connections to the school. First of all, Mom Ronson's mother's house was still there; she had it built on the campus. She had "willed" it over to Mom at her passing, so the Ronsons could move there when they retired from the ministry. Then another house became available for rent on campus, so the door opened for us to be close to where Mom and Dad Ronson would eventually be.

Furthermore, over the years Dad Ronson had come to know several retired missionaries living on the school property. They came to visit us from time to time. Being with them further stirred my calling to Christian ministry.

My wife, Nora, was also inspired to go back to school. She wanted to study journalism, so, in considering TFC, we both felt it was the place for us, and everything we saw on the horizon looked like blue skies, sunshine, and roses.

GETTING DOWN TO BUSINESS

When we arrived, we decided Nora would enroll in school first because she wanted to get her schooling out of the way. Then she could support me while I attended. That would also give me a chance to work and get ourselves financially established. Actually, we had no idea how we would afford the expense of college and raise three children too. But the Lord paved the way for me to be the Director of Maintenance for the school. My job was to care for all the physical operations of the 1,100-acre campus, and it fitted me well.

Nora had a very heavy academic load and threw herself into her studies. I'd help her a little at night with memory verses and such. She was a wonderful student and I was really proud of her. She had left that old messed up life of drugs and alcohol behind, and was now at the top of her class; she was one of only two others to make the Dean's list by mid-term. That was a great accomplishment.

We didn't have a lot of money, and it was scary at times because my salary was now one-quarter of what I used to earn at Daniel Construction, but God took care of us. He provided for all our needs and filled us with unspeakable joy.

So, it was an O.K. plan. The only thing that gnawed at me was that the call of ministry was burning in me so strongly that I didn't know how I was going to wait four years for my turn to be a student. Unfortunately, my wait to start school wasn't something I had to worry about for very long. A dramatic change was coming. We had been in Toccoa for only a few months when a terrible tragedy struck the campus. I'll never forget the day it happened. It will be etched in my mind forever.

CHAPTER THIRTEEN

I HEARD THE TRAIN COMING

We were shopping in town one evening, going from store to store. Our last stop was J.C. Penny, where Jaimée found and fell in love with a little red plastic, riding-horse with yellow wheels. She got on that thing, wrapped her little legs around it, and would not let go! Everyone in the store was amused. I had to lift her and the horse up onto the counter so the clerk could scan the bar code under her little behind. We purchased that plus several other items. Then we ran through the parking lot in the rain to where the car was and made our way home.

There was a lot of rain that week; it had rained every day for ten days. By the time we got to the cemetery at the top of the hill on Falls Road, the rain was coming down in torrents. I'm sure you've driven in rain so heavy that the wipers couldn't keep up. That's what we had encountered that night.

For as far as we could see, all the street lights suddenly went out. So we pulled over to the side of the road and waited quite a while, hoping to get a break in the weather. Finally, we saw that it wasn't going to let up, so we launched out again, inching our way home in the dark.

In the distance, we saw huge flashes of light over the campus but it wasn't lightning. When we got to the campus we saw that all the lights were out there too.

We all piled into the house and started looking for candles to light our way. It was near bedtime so Nora and I settled the children into their beds, but of course, Jaimée had to have a few quick spins through the house on her new little riding horse.

We left all the bedroom doors open and dragged our coffee table into the hallway to serve as a candle stand so we could see our way to the bathroom in the night. I put a big fat candle on it. The flicker from the wick danced to the music of the rain drumming on the roof. Nora went to our room and I followed shortly afterward. I lay down and managed to drop off quickly, yet somehow, my sleep was fitful.

THE TRAIN
Then, about 1:30 in the morning, I woke up to the sound of a "passing train". I listened for a few seconds and sat up. It really did sound like a train. Still half asleep I shuffled over to the window and tried to focus on what was going on outside.

There in the far distance in the dark, I saw something kind of long, moving toward us from a sideways position. It looked like the broad side of a locomotive. Mmm. I was still trying to figure it out when I noticed my feet were wet. Then, becoming more awake, I realized we didn't have a train track within miles of where we were! At that point, I knew something was terribly wrong.

I tried to control my panic. I called my wife's name and the names of all my children. I said, "Come on, get up! Everybody, get up. Something's wrong. I think the creek has overflowed and the water's coming in the house! Get up; get up!"

Now the water was really beginning to come in. It was up to my knees and quickly rising, which had extinguished the candle. So in the darkness, I found the coffee table and yanked it over a few feet to position it under the attic scuttle hole. There was no rope attached to the pull-down stairs so I stood on the coffee table and began digging at the ceiling with my fingers to find the edge of the attic door.

With broken, bleeding fingernails I got the door open and pulled the ladder down. I heard my oldest son yelling, "Dad help! Dad, it's a tornado! Help me!" But I didn't know where he was.

I grabbed my wife--she was holding the baby in her arms--and pushed both of them up the ladder into the attic. I didn't think the water would rise that high.

I turned to my left where my daughter's bedroom was. She stood on her bed and screamed. When I got to her the water was almost to my neck. I grabbed her and headed back toward the hallway. I pushed her up, hoping she could also make it into the attic, but by then I was underwater, so I didn't realize I had only managed to crush her up against the frame of her bedroom door. Then everything went black. I was swallowed by the water and swept away.

THE DAM

There was a water dam in the hills above the college. It had originally been built in 1899 to create a reservoir for a waterfall-driven hydroelectric power plant. That plant supplied power to the city of Toccoa. Then in 1933, Georgia power took over and the college kept the energy supply for itself.

An earthen dam was built around 1940. After World War II, the dam height was again raised, creating a 40-acre lake. Finally, in 1957, the use of water power for producing electricity was stopped.

So there it stood 38 feet high, 400 feet long, and 20 feet thick. With each heavy rainfall, the water levels rose, the pressure of the lake behind it increased, and the dam got weaker, until 1:30 in the morning, November 6, 1977, when it gave way and took 39 lives.

The Army Corps of Engineers reported that the wall of water that rushed over the broken dam was 55 feet high, and traveled at a speed of 110 miles per hour as it raced through the campus valley. It mercilessly cleared everything in its path.

IMPOSSIBLE WORLD

I have no idea how much time passed but I do have a few scanty memories. For example, while I was fighting to put Nora and Jaimée into the attic, I remember glancing at all the pictures and diplomas hanging neatly on the wall and how they became airborne, flying toward me like missals. Also, the library had become animated as hundreds of books danced and churned in the water.

I remember how the walls began to break. In fact, the whole structure of the house broke apart, splitting away from its foundation, and sweeping me away at a terrible speed under the water.

It was overwhelming and I wish I could describe every detail. What I can say is there was no other world for me except this cold, spinning, centrifuge of rushing water. There was no more school, no freight train, no automobiles, no factories, no clothing stores, no roads or houses; just a crazy, impossible world I found myself trapped in. It made no sense.

SAVING GRACE

I don't remember much of anything else until I felt my head slam into something solid and hard. I wrapped my arms around it and clung to it for my very life. I wasn't moving anymore but everything else continued to swirl past me, jabbing me along its way.

I couldn't figure out what I hit, but it was smooth and tall and stationary. Still, under water, I felt my way along the object, clinging to it with all my strength. I don't know how long I had been holding my breath, and I wasn't sure which way was up or down. None-the-less, I began to climb this *thing,* hoping I would find a way out.

Then I reached the surface and found air. Moments passed before I could clear my head and get my bearings. At that point, it dawned on me: I was clinging to the mast of a forklift! It was the only thing in my present world that wasn't moving and I thanked God for leading me to it.

I don't know how long I stayed there, clinging to the top of that machine. The water continued to surge by me, threatening to rip me from the security of its greasy, steel mast. I also remember how the darkness of the night enveloped me. It was cruel and terrorizing. It held me in some sort of nether-land, and I imagined that all my family was lost; gone forever. What was I supposed to do now?

Shaking me out of my train of thought, I heard a crying sound, like that of a child, alone and afraid. But where was it coming from? Was I hearing things? Was it real or was it not?

CHAPTER FOURTEEN

A BUBBLE OF AIR

It seemed to take forever, but the water level finally receded somewhat. Above the gushing sounds, my ears continued to follow the talking and crying I had heard off to my left. I wanted to find whoever was out there.

Just then, some 55-gallon barrels were swirling around me and I thought I could ride one of them over to the sound source. Instead, I decided to simply jump in and swim. As I got closer to it, I saw something popping out through the surface of the water. It was the top part of the cab of a big army truck we used for the maintenance department. The top few inches of the window were above the water through which I could see a tiny figure. It was my son, Kirk.

I guess Kirk found the truck in the nick of time, because trapped under its canvas roof, was a large and sufficient bubble of air for him to breathe until the water level could inch its way back down. As I swam over to him, I heard him crying, "Thank you God for the water. Thank you God for the flood." And I was amazed.

As a young believer, he was obedient in giving thanks in *all* things. Saturday, just hours before, we had studied in First Thessalonians, chapter five, which says we should give thanks in everything that happens, no matter what it is. That's just what Kirk was doing. He told me he was cold, and he was afraid that no one was left alive, so he was talking to God about jumping back into the water. He just wanted to go to Heaven to be with us. Thank *God* I found him when I did!

I tore the canvas top from the truck and wrapped him in it. The force of the water had torn away our clothes. It was more powerful than you could imagine. I also found a pair of old khaki cut-offs just my waist size that I was able to put on to cover my own nakedness.

Kirk and I huddled together, there in that old Army truck, and waited until the waters went down to a depth that allowed us to start walking. We made our way to higher ground where some mobile homes were. They had remained intact as they were above the water level. Paul Stacey lived in one of the homes. I met up with him and he gave me a pair of shoes that fit me, (wow), and a flashlight. I was grateful. The only thing to do now was to look for more people who had survived.

DID YOU SEE HER?

So I began walking the path of the flood-plain, not knowing what to expect. Not too far ahead I saw a group of about a dozen people gathered together sitting by the creek bank, and behind them, I saw others emerge from piles of broken homes, cars, concrete, and tree limbs. A woman was being carried out on a make-shift stretcher. I stopped them and aimed my flashlight at her. I could see she was badly broken, her face was swollen, purple, and blue, and was covered with mud and bits of debris. She was unrecognizable due to the damage she had sustained. I thought it would be a miracle if she lived, and I said, "That woman will make it to Heaven before she ever makes it to a hospital."

As I got closer to the little group, I was amazed to discover my other son and daughter, Doug and Anita. Anita said she had managed to land on a small

71

portion of a roof that had broken loose from a house. She stayed afloat on it throughout the terrible ordeal. And while being swept away, she said she heard a woman crying and realized it was her mom!

She continued, "Daddy, I was so glad to hear Mom's voice that I left the piece of roof and paddled over to her, hoping she was O.K. But she was tangled up in something; it was part of a barbed wire fence I think. Anyway, it took me a little while but I got her free, and then help came." She began to sob, "Oh, Daddy, she's badly hurt, they just took her away on a stretcher. Did you see her?"

I felt myself choking out the words, "My God! A stretcher? You mean the woman I just saw being carried out was her?!" I couldn't say any more. I had to find out about my wife. How serious was she, I wondered. Will she survive? After asking everyone I met, I was told she was taken to Stephens County Hospital.

THE AFTERMATH BEGINS

Before I left for the hospital, I first had to fix a *little* problem for the people I was with. Like me and Kirk, many of the folks barely had any clothing left on their bodies, due to the force of the water. It had ripped everything off of us. Furthermore, the chill of the early November morning was taking its toll.

I remembered that Mom and Dad Ronson's house was on the edge of the campus, near our house and the creek. I thought if we could all make it over there, we could possibly find clothing, food, and rest. I told the little group of about a dozen to follow me and we would see if the house was still there.

We all walked along together, picking our way through the darkness, stumbling over broken pieces of

R. Douglas Veer

this and that, while the mud sucked at our feet and legs with every step. I knew the house wasn't very far, yet the journey was long and tiresome. Finally, as we rounded the corner, there stood the house. Although it was knocked off of its foundation, only two or three feet of water surrounded it, so it was quite accessible. It was our refuge in this horribly traumatic time, and we were thankful.

Does God take care of his own? Watch this: after I broke the front door window, I reached through and unlocked the door. We all went inside, and just as a stupid gesture, I picked up the telephone. The entire campus was without electricity, gas, or water, but when I lifted the phone I heard, "*bz-z-z*". It worked! How was that even possible? But it did!!

I told everyone to call their family, no matter how far away they lived, and let them know that they were alright. I ask you again, "Does God take care of His own?" You be the judge; I know what I believe.

I can't remember exactly how the days unfolded from there, but I had gone back to the valley, the disaster site, either later that day or the next. It was all so surreal. By then, the water levels had diminished and were back within the banks of the tiny, rippling creek-bed. There were massive piles of debris everywhere as bulldozers, backhoes, and trucks were attempting to clean away all evidence of the catastrophe.

I walked through the aftermath, combing and searching; picking up bits and pieces of family treasures that were now worthless trash. I hoped I might find an item or two that belonged to me, and I thought about my daughter, Jaimée. I knew she was with the Lord, but I felt pain as well as blessing. I was blessed knowing that because of His great love and mercy, she was with God. We have the assurance according to Scripture, that all young children are immediately in the presence of Jesus at the moment of death. Yet, I could not deny the pain I felt over losing her. I knew it would take an unknown amount of time to reconcile that into my everyday life.

CHAPTER FIFTEEN

A DOUBLE PROMISE

The ten days of torrential rains were over and the morning delivered a brilliant, clear sky. As I walked along the creek-bank, searching for whatever possessions were left for those who had survived, I glanced up into the blue and I was stunned! There, in all the glory God created was a double rainbow stretching from the horizon on the left to the horizon on the right.

We read in Genesis, chapter nine about the great destructive flood that covered the earth. When it had ended, God sent a sign in the form of a rainbow and promised mankind that He would never again cause the earth and its people to be destroyed by water.

That morning, God sent a majestic, double promise! He sent a double rainbow to assure us. And I stood in awe of its appearance.

IT IS WELL WITH MY SOUL

There's so much to tell about the dam break in Georgia that occurred November 6, 1977; volumes could be written. Thirty-nine people lost their lives that night, and the lives of many families were changed forever. But, it's not for me to say why things happened the way they did. All I know is, God is in control and He allows certain things for a reason.

We must remember, this world is not paradise. Far from it. According to the Bible, this world is run by Satan, the ruler of darkness.

When Adam sinned in the Garden of Eden, he gave up the benefits of Paradise. He traded his peace with God for the right to do whatever he pleased. All people born since then have had the freedom to choose between right or wrong. It's called *free will*, and unfortunately, it's that free will that gets us into so much trouble.

We make wrong choices and act selfishly, even though others might suffer because of it. We make mistakes and fall short of the glory of God which is something He intended us to have. That's why God sent His Son, Jesus, to help us. God knew we needed a Savior, and oh, what a caring Savior He is! I praise the Lord because Jesus is my Savior. I live on the winning side of freedom and that's why, even amidst all of this, I can still sing, "It is well with my soul!"

JAIMÉE

Many of my friends passed away on that cold November night. I'm so glad I know where they are. They're safe and secure with the Lord. Having that full assurance is what has brought me through the stormy waters, the looming aftermath, the mud, and the mire. It's a comfort to know that all is well with them.

As for our precious 21-month-old Jaimée, God allowed her to go home and be with Him. I know deep in my soul that she is at peace. I know she's having a wonderful time and loving every minute of it. I imagine her peering tenderly into the eyes of Jesus as He holds her in His loving arms. I can picture her smiling and touching His beard with her soft, gentle hand, saying, "Zeesus; Zeesus."

I expect I will be able to hold Jaimée in my arms again one day. Her little fingers will touch my face as she greets me saying, "Daddy, welcome to Heaven." Then I expect I'll turn to Jesus--face to face--and thank Him for taking care of my little girl. I'm so glad He is always present with all the children in Heaven. Quite honestly, that's exactly where I want to be as well.

THE OTHER SIDE OF HOPE

After the tragedy, there came the personal interviews, the radio shows, the newspaper reporters, and the magazine articles. We had speaking engagements all around the country and we were "the people of the hour", so-to-speak. But when the hoopla died down, Nora and I were faced with the arduous task of putting our lives back together again.

People came from New York and other faraway cities to offer counseling services. Such was available to the survivors, free of charge. I now must sadly say, every single one of us walked away from the opportunity. Why the strange and regrettable response? Because the President of the college, Dr. Kenneth Opperman, had some skewed ideas about Christian doctrine.

Instead of encouraging us to get assistance, he challenged us to reject it. He said, "You are Christians, and God is your counselor. You don't need psychological counseling. That's not for Christian people. You should rely on God alone. I *dare* you to receive counsel from the world!"

How do you suppose we felt after hearing that? How could we seek help? It would have been shameful. We were hurting from a pain we couldn't understand, or control; a pain for which we couldn't find healing. Yet, we were being ordered by our leader to avoid getting the support we needed!

I think it was the cruelest thing that could have been done to us, especially coming from the College President. (He was a mere bystander in this tragedy, by the way.)

To the best of my knowledge, every surviving married couple except one is now divorced. A prison of despair was created that night and many are still in that prison. Just a side note: today, in the aftermath of it all, the college now has a degree program in psychology and counseling.

WASHED AWAY

Soon, we left the school and moved to Tuscaloosa, Alabama, where Mom and Dad Ronson had taken another church. So we went to help them but as much as I liked the city, I was never at peace there. None-the-less, we stayed a couple of years and then moved with them to Columbus, Mississippi, to do the same thing for another two years.

It turns out we couldn't adjust there either. First of all, Nora's old haunts had come back. She feared God would *never* let her have children again. Secondly, between the trauma of being trapped under water for so long, and having her face crushed, her neck broken, and her leg broken, she had a lot to overcome. Adding to all that, she was still suffering over losing Jaimée. Nora was at her limit; she couldn't take any more and we really needed to find our happiness again.

Yes, losing Jaimée was the greatest trauma of all. Nora so needed to be healed from that. It remained *the* source of her sorrow and that grief began to erode our marriage.

When Jaimée went out of our lives, I think the love that Nora had for me left as well. She never returned to that happy person I needed. *That* Nora was washed away and buried along with all our personal belongings and treasures, now hidden deep beneath the soil of Toccoa Falls. That chapter in our lives had ended, and we couldn't seem to get on with the rest of the book.

CHAPTER SIXTEEN

A LITTLE SUNSHINE

Without accepting the counseling that was offered, Nora and I managed to plod ahead. Eventually, joy *did* come in the way of two wonderful, God-given gifts. The first was Amanda Faith, born October 2, 1978. The second was Hope Ronson, born August 31, 1980.

I never thought it would be possible to love a child again as much as I loved Jaimée, but it happened, and it was a sweet victory. It was as if God was holding all of Jaimée's love in a bank for us to draw interest. Then, when our girls were born, God let us withdraw it to pour over them. Our cups were running over and a ray of hope shone down on us. I loved all my children, but I had a very special place in my heart for these two daughters, gifted to us to help fill the void and bring healing. Even now, as grown adults, they will always be Daddy's little girls.

A ROOT OF HOPE

I thought our lives would finally get back to normal with these two precious children. I thought Nora and I would grow old together and share many memories. I thought we had weathered all the disasters a person could have in a lifetime, and I thought we could put our hurts and heartaches behind us forever, but I was wrong. Another lesson was yet to be learned: never look into your future expecting to know the outcome.

We can't change the past, and tomorrow is never promised. There are no guarantees that all will go well.

We can only take the present day and do our best with it. We can only appreciate the now and ask God to give us His grace for the 'morrow. We must put our energies into being what we're supposed to be and spend ourselves in the giving of kindness, patience, understanding, and every other good thing we can offer. We need God to bathe us daily in His love for when we realize how much God loves us, only then can we truly love others.

We, humans, are miserable creatures without the Lord. On our own, our final outcome will be disastrous. We are self-centered and cling to our rights even when we know we're in the wrong. We continue in our sinful pride on the pathway to failure.

It was that human element in me that caused my life to break down again. Even so, I clung to a root of hope in God Almighty. God is not changeable like we are. He is our solid rock and our firm foundation.

BACK TO TOCCOA

Nora and I had many problems coming out of the dam break. For one thing, we were living in the past, yearning for the early days when we were happy. We wanted to recapture that but we just couldn't get back to the way things were. It was like trying to find a long lost coin or bring back a fading dream. Even so, we wanted to try.

That's why we elected to move back to Toccoa. I felt we had unfinished business there: we needed to face our fears caused by the tragedy, and, try to draw closer together. If Nora and I were going to find each other again, this would be the place to do it. So we took a stab at it knowing it wasn't going to be easy. Things had changed for us; something was lost, but was it lost forever?

Another problem was that the spiritual commitment I had when we were on campus was gone. I no longer had that wonderful joy of serving God. I guess my joy was destroyed in the flood waters and carried away. So I went on without it, for I didn't have the power to bring it back.

THE BUSINESS OF "WORK"

Time marched on. I missed the way Nora and I used to share every part of our lives together. But she just wasn't spending time at home anymore. Up until now, she had been a homemaker; she loved her home life. But now she didn't want to be around the house. Now she was demanding that God provide her with a job. She became obsessed with the idea of going to work.

Well, she got exactly what she asked for, and I had to pick up the slack. In addition to my working construction, I had to take over the domestic chores.

As the months rolled by, Nora's job came to be an ever-increasing part of her life. The family became less and less important. I personally felt that if I had dropped off the face of the earth I wouldn't have been missed.

I was attending church alone, caring for the kids alone, and trying to keep up a spiritual life alone. Finally, I thought, "If you can't beat 'em, join 'em". So I started putting more time in at work myself and put Nora at the bottom of my priority list. Work gave me a greater sense of being, anyway, and I needed that.

Sadly, even if she *had* reached out more with her emotional needs, I'm not sure that I would have responded. There was an emotional disconnect between us. Instead of being patient with her, I would curse at her and then go into deep remorse before the

Lord. And just when I thought my troubles were resolved, I found myself at it again.

Through it all, my wife developed nervous tension and severe panic attacks. The more she worsened, the less I *felt* for her inexcusable weaknesses. I thought, if she just made up her mind and got a grip, she'd be O.K. but it wasn't that simple. Much of her stress was actually coming from her job and that worked against us in our home life. So we scheduled ourselves to stay out of each other's way.

WHAT'S LOVE GOT TO DO WITH IT?

I still loved my wife but we had walls between us. We should have immediately investigated to see who the brick mason was, so-to-speak. Brick upon brick was set in place. The anger between us grew, leading to a huge stockpile of hurtful stones. The wall of indifference and uncaring grew stronger and higher, separating us from each other.

God is not in the business of building walls; He builds bridges. Walls come from pride and selfishness and must be kept in check. Walls are the sign of the Devil's best handiwork. Allowing walls to grow is an open invitation for the Devil to raise havoc in our lives.

We saw each other, we were near each other, we were with each other, yet we weren't really together. I began to hate our life, and resent my wife, and that was just the tip of the iceberg.

I know it sounds terrible, especially coming from a man who professes Godly principles, but I was fresh out of those principles. And so, we were like two ships passing in the night. We were aware of each other's existence, but that was about it.

Looking back, hindsight is always 20/20. Maybe I could have put more into the marriage, but of course, it would have taken both of us. I don't think she was willing to work at it. She wanted her freedom. So all I could do was catalog it under *experience,* and draw upon it in the future. Hopefully, sharing this with you will keep you from falling into the same sort of pitfall. Otherwise, it will have all been a tragic waste of experience.

CHAPTER SEVENTEEN

DAD RONSON'S FINAL HOUR

Just when I really needed a best friend, another loss came my way. The time had come for my (adopted) Dad's final hour. Dad Ronson spent his last 12 days in a nursing home. And I remember the last of those days so well.

He was comfortably situated in his bed, ready to read his Bible. The nurse had just brought him a hot cup of coffee and propped him up so he could take a sip now and then, and go back to his reading. This had become a frequent and favorite past time of his. It was also known throughout the hospital that he often shared his spiritual findings with the various nurses that cared for him.

On this particular day, a certain nurse had brought Dad his drink and then came back a few minutes later to check on him. She asked him if his drink was hot enough, and he mentioned that actually, it could have been heated up a bit more. She cheerfully returned it to the kitchen to refresh it for him, when at that very moment, Dad simply passed away.

When the nurse came back with his drink, she noticed his head was down and the Bible had fallen to his chest. Her first thought was that he had fallen asleep. She imagined straightening him up to make him more comfortable. But when she approached him . . . she realized he was gone.

After Dad's funeral, Mom Ronson shared something very special with me. Dad used to tell me that if a person lived an entire lifetime and had only one true friend, that person will have died a wealthy man. Mom told me Dad had said I was the only true friend he ever had. I was very humbled by those words; I felt so unworthy of them. But I accepted them as an expression of his true love for me.

As for the Bible Dad treasured so much--the one he was reading at the moment he died--Mom gave that Bible to me. She knew Dad and I had a bond and that having his Bible would mean a lot to me. It did, and it still does.

I'm telling you this, not to boast, but to show you how God can change lives; even one like mine. Yes, God had given me, Pastor, Dad Ronson as an advisor, but He also gave me a wonderful friend. Today, if I could speak to him I would say, "I miss you Dad. Please keep a place close by up there for me because one day soon, I'll be coming to be with you again."

Dad Ronson went home to be with the Lord, September 23, 1992. My heart truly grieved at his passing and I have missed him terribly. I wish I could have absorbed and applied more of what he shared. But I'm grateful for all that he instilled in me.

SETTLING INTO MY HOME-LIFE

My life continued with my family. I typically spent my evenings in the kitchen cooking supper. That is, I would get off of work early enough to get Hope from the Happy Corner Day Care. Then I'd pick up Amanda from her first-grade class with Mrs. Bumgardner and my evening routine would unfold from there. Nora would come home sometime later and we'd all have supper together.

Some nights, of course, Nora would either come home much later, or she'd stop in only to return to work and stay late. Sometimes it was 11:30 or midnight before she finally got in. She worked at the local hospital as a patient advocate advisor. Although she got to the office at the same time each day, her hours were otherwise very irregular. I never questioned her schedule because she seemed so happy, and I had my own home building business to take care of. I thought we were both on a pretty good upward career-climb to success.

MIND GAMES IN MY HOUSE

We had experienced a few confrontations because of my old jealous nature. Additionally, I had been physically hurt on the job and so I was taking huge amounts of Motrin to control the inflammation in my knee. Somehow, Nora convinced me that one of the side effects of Motrin was paranoia (which would explain my jealous behavior). Nora's job gave her access to a book called a P.D.R., used by medical professionals to determine the effects of drugs. So I succumbed to her Motrin theory. I didn't want to, but I accepted it as being true.

One particular night, it occurred to me that things just didn't feel right, and it wasn't just my paranoia. Nora was home much earlier than usual and she had an air of uneasiness about her. As I puttered around in the kitchen I felt an increasingly strong presence of danger. I wondered if I was picking up something Nora had brought home with her. I asked her a couple of questions and let her know I thought something was wrong. Finally, she told me she had lost her job.

I thought about our financial situation and the loss of our second income, but I quickly replaced that idea with my concern for her. I knew her job was very important to her and I wondered how this would affect

87

her emotionally. She had already been battling with anxiety for the last six or seven months, and now this. But there was more . . .

Nora had been seeing a female psychiatrist at the hospital who had prescribed some very strong medication for her called Ativan. It was supposed to help control her panic attacks. About a month after she started taking it, the doctor told her the drug was addictive and she'd require controlled hospitalization to wean her off of it. What could we do? By then, it was too late.

I wanted to jump in and help, so I looked into her job situation. Wouldn't it be great if I could help restore that part of her life that she loved so much? But when I got to the bottom of the matter I realized the problem wasn't her state of mental health. It was something else entirely.

Nora finally told me there were *rumors* floating around the hospital that she and another employee had been behaving improperly at work. (They were having an affair.) She said they were both dismissed from their jobs to protect the image of the hospital.

FAIR IS FAIR!

Wow! How could it be? I just didn't believe it. All I could say was, "look out world!" I was fighting mad at the hospital for hurting Nora's feelings and her reputation!! I tried to comfort her, and in the midst of my anger, I told her I would go to the administrator to see to it that this matter appeared before the hospital board of directors. She deserved a full and fair explanation for this kind of treatment, and so did her coworker. That night I comforted her in the best way I could.

In the days ahead my anger rose to the boiling point. I thought, "After all Nora has done for them and look how they've acted toward her!" I reflected on the many nights she had worked late. And when she did I would often cook up a big pot of stew or spaghetti and take it down to everyone on the shift. We both had literally poured ourselves into that place.

To me, the whole thing was blatant abuse on their part, to treat my darling Nora that way. She had been through enough in this life to last two lifetimes. It was time for me to stand in the gap for my beloved one. I wanted to be the manly husband Nora needed and deserved.

I thought, "Hell hath no fury like a woman scorned" and even *that* Hell was going to pale alongside the protection I would give my wife. She needed me now more than ever since she didn't have the strength to stand up for herself, so I thought. Look out Stephens County Hospital! Here comes the wrath of a husband scorned over an injured wife; a wife very dearly loved; one for whom I was willing to lay down my life.

CHAPTER EIGHTEEN

THE PLOT BEGINS TO BOIL

A meeting was set up for the next day. I imagined all the things that might be said "on the morrow" and so I slept very fitfully that night. Strangely though, I had my own suspicions about what happened. I found myself doubting Nora's story, but then I felt ashamed. I simply had to protect her. She was my darling and she had promised me she had been truthful. So why was I having a problem with that? Would my deepest fear come true? Or was my alleged Motrin-based paranoia just something to cover up her lies?

I was frightened and I prayed, "God, how can this be happening to me? How can our lives be in turmoil again? Haven't we been through enough?" I lay there thinking; my doubts were swimming around in my head like a big school of fish. My mind was flooded with thoughts too numerous to organize.

Something else: Nora made a statement that rang in my head. She said she and this man had actually been accused once of being caught in a sexual situation. They received two weeks probation for it as a reprimand. Impossible! Wouldn't I have known about that?

I heard other stories too. It was said that they had met at Calaway Gardens near Atlanta for a weekend fling. It was also said that they both took their wedding rings off when at work each day; they put them in their desk drawers. It was a symbol of their devotion to each other. Oh yeah, and *he* was the guy that sent her the unsigned birthday card, professing his love.

It was all so inconceivable, yet, they had been caught again, less than two weeks into their probation. I wanted to deny every detail. I said, "Not my precious, darling wife. No, God. It can't be true; it just can't be! Can it?"

Sleep escaped me. All sorts of images ran through my head, The night was long and torturous but I didn't want the morning to come either. I didn't want to see what the day would bring.

As a child, I use to have a recurring nightmare. I saw myself running endlessly but never finding refuge because I was lost and didn't know where I was. I did know there was a monster trying to catch me, but I didn't know how to get away from it. I didn't know it then but *this* monster was about to catch me. It was ready for me, right in the middle of the board meeting, at the hospital, the very next day.

THE STEW THICKENS

I couldn't even guess why Nora had allowed this meeting to take place. She knew what she had done. Surely she knew she couldn't hide the facts. Thinking back, perhaps she thought she was more clever than she actually was. Perhaps she thought she could bluff her way through, or that I wouldn't really go with her. Never-the-less, we went to the meeting as planned.

The appointed time had arrived. We all filed into the conference room and I took my place at one end of the table; the administrator sat at the other end. Nora was to my right and the other guilty party was across from her. There were a couple of others present as well.

The administrator opened. "I understand you have come here today to examine the personnel files of Nora and Mr.___; however, since I've talked to both of

91

them, they have declined their permission to discuss this matter. Therefore, I am bound by law to . . ."

I interrupted with, "Now wait just a minute! You said you would open their personnel files for us." Then, turning to Nora I said, "Just half an hour ago you said you would go through with this. What's going on here?"

There was a pause. Neither of them answered. I said it again. "You came here today to look at the records, so we could prove error on the part of the hospital. Here we are. Now, what's going on?"

Nora spoke quietly with, "I've changed my mind." Then Mr. ____ said, "Me too."

The administrator repeated, "I'm sorry, but by law, I have to honor their wishes. I'm afraid this meeting is over."

Everyone rose from the table. The assistants left the room. That left me and Mr. ____ and Nora and the chief. I turned to Mr. ____ and said, "That's O.K. I guess I'll just settle this my way!" I started toward him, but he quickly moved around the long conference table to get away from me. I chased him one way around the table, and then the other. Finally, he grabbed hold of Nora by the back of the shoulders and used her to shield himself from me while he backed up near the door and slipped away.

So the whole meeting just fizzled out. Nora and I gathered our senses and went home. That night, our normally peaceful household was not a pleasant place to be. We did get around to talking about the matter and Nora said, "It was really Mr. ____ who had changed his mind about exposing his own personnel file, not me". She pleaded, "What could I say or do? It wasn't my fault."

Of course, she assured me there had been no relationship with that man, and she completely denied her involvement and guilt. Case closed. The conversation ended and once again, I was faced with trying to put our lives back together. Yes, I wanted us to get on the right track but all I could do was hash over everything from the past few months. Nothing made sense to me; I was so confused.

SO TIRED

Yes, I was confused and tired. How I wished things could be simple again like they were years ago. I thought about how the Bible teaches simplicity, purity, and innocence. I thought about how children fit into this context; how they never get bogged down in life's complexities; how they seem unscathed by hurts and lies and deceit. Even the simple act of coming to Jesus is done without reservation. They receive the plain simple truth in a spirit of trust.

I was truly tired of the rat-race. I thought I didn't care anymore, yet deep down inside I did care, and I longed to be comforted. Peace alluded me though and I just felt lost.

Not so long ago, times were better and the people in my world were better, like Miss Lucy in Dallas. To me, she was a shining example of what a Christian woman should be.

Jesus said, **"Verily I say unto you, Whosoever shall not receive the kingdom of God as a little child shall in no wise enter therein,"** (Luke 18:17).

Miss Lucy portrayed the very meaning of this Scripture, even though she was in her 80s. She put herself to work in God's field to reap a harvest of lives, leading people to salvation in Jesus. I'm so glad she reached me before it was too late. I loved her for it and appreciated her so much. Her simplicity and faithfulness were a tremendous witness to many!

CHAPTER NINETEEN

CATCHING UP WITH MISS LUCY

I thought about Miss Lucy so much that I decided to call her and apologize. I had put her through a lot during those many visits she made, inviting me to church. My dirty street language and rude manners were extremely hurtful and I was sure I had offended her. That was who I was back then. I was a long-haired, pot smoking, pill popping, foul-mouthed rebel. I was lost and on my way to Hell.

Then Jesus got a hold of me thanks to Miss Lucy. I wanted her to know her efforts had not been wasted. I had gone on with the Lord and I was changed.

I called information in Dallas and asked for the telephone number for Lucille Lancaster. I was really surprised when the operator gave it to me! After all these years I actually managed to find her again. I was amazed she was even alive; she must have been nearing a hundred years old!

She answered the phone and I could tell immediately she was still spry and alert because she recognized my voice instantly.

"Miss Lucy?" I asked.

"Yes . . . this is Lucille . . . can I help you?" she pleasantly inquired.

"Miss Lucy . . . I'm not sure that you'll remember me, but, well . . . this is . . ."

"Oh . . . why, yes! Why Doug-o-las," she declared. "Yes, of course. I couldn't forget one of my children. How are you? It's wonderful to hear from you!"

It was so nice to hear her voice again. We chatted awhile about all that had happened over the years. Then I got serious and said, "Miss Lucy, I called because I want to say just one thing to you about those many Saturdays you came to visit. Well, I just wanted you to know how sorry I am for all the trouble I caused you and for all the rude language and poor manners I showed you. I just wanted to say that . . ."

She gently interrupted, saying, "Why Doug-o-las, you never did any such thing!" At that moment, I knew she had long since forgiven me and truly loved me with the love of God. In fact, I'll never forget how she loved me right into the submission of our Lord with the sweetest heart of Jesus I've ever known.

We talked a little more and then said our goodbyes. At the time of this writing, I now must report that Lucille has gone on to be with Jesus. I'm so glad I had the chance to talk with her one last time, and thank her for witnessing Christ to me.

Is there someone in your life you might like to call and thank? It would be a good thing to do before they're gone and the opportunity is lost. Also, if you haven't shared what Christ has done for you, you need to get busy. Miss Lucy was such a great example. We should all try to be "Miss Lucys" to the world around us because we never know what tomorrow might bring.

THE BEGINNING OF THE END

As important as Miss Lucy was to me, I supposed that my wife's father was equally important to her. So when she told me he had suddenly become ill, I knew she was probably quite concerned. Following that, Nora announced that she would be going to see her dad in Pennsylvania. At the same time, that's when things really started falling apart.

You see, she told me that her father was about to have emergency brain surgery and she wanted to be with him. What good husband would have not let her go? Yes, I was understanding of the situation and I released her without question.

Guess what? She never returned. She just copped an excuse, and a good one I might add. Furthermore, after she left she subsequently filed for divorce.

The deputy sheriff who was supposed to serve me my divorce papers was a friend of mine. He would look for me every day at each of my four jobs. But my employees always helped me; they would watch for him and tell me he was coming. Then I'd hide.

He must have figured out I was being tipped off. I did give him quite the run-around but I didn't want a divorce. To me, divorce was worse than a death sentence. When I saw it looming on the horizon, I wanted to avoid the paperwork as long as I could.

I wanted to work things out with Nora and save the family. I was hoping she would accept my forgiveness and see I was offering my understanding of what had happened. We spoke on the phone a couple of times and I felt she was leaning in that direction. She once even had me go 75 miles to meet her at an airport so we could "talk"; she was supposedly flying in there. She led me to believe she was coming home. But it never happened.

R. Douglas Veer

ALONE AGAIN, NATURALLY
(Writer: Gilbert O' Sullivan)

In a little while from now
If I'm not feeling any less sour
I promise myself to treat myself
And visit a nearby tower

And climbing to the top, will throw myself off
In an effort to make it clear
To whoever what it's like when you're shattered
Left standing in the lurch at a church

Where people saying, "My God, that's tough
She's stood him up no point in us remaining
We may as well go home"
As I did on my own alone again, naturally

To think that only yesterday
I was cheerful, bright and gay
Looking forward to well who wouldn't do
The role I was about to play

But as if to knock me down reality came around
And without so much, as a mere touch
Cut me into little pieces leaving me to doubt

Talk about God in His mercy
Who if He really does exist
Why did he desert me in my hour of need
I truly am indeed, alone again, naturally

It seems to me that there are more hearts
Broken in the world that can't be mended
Left unattended; What do we do? What do we do?
Alone again, naturally

97

Now looking back over the years
And whatever else that appears
I remember I cried when my father died
Never wishing to hide the tears

And at sixty-five years old
My mother, God rest her soul
Couldn't understand why the only man
She had ever loved had been taken

Leaving her to start with a heart so badly broken
Despite encouragement from me
No words were ever spoken and when she passed away
I cried and cried all day, alone again, naturally
Alone again, naturally

I'm not sure if it was her or the folks on Nora's end of the line who talked her out of reconciling with me. Maybe I just wanted to give her the benefit of the doubt but I still question it. Why is it that folks feel they have to meddle in the lives of others? Why do some people stick their noses in where they don't belong? Don't they realize that marriage and family are sacred grounds, not to be ruined by those who have no stake in it?

I could never understand all the marriage advice going around, especially from those who were unmarried! They lead people to outcomes they don't want and fill their minds with prejudices and half-truths.

And what about the marriage vows: " Let no man put asunder . . ." Don't people realize that breaking a godly vow can never bring peace? Our most important relationship is with God, not people, so unless God has the final say in our decisions, we're doomed.

With great hindsight, I now admit that waiting on God to lead me through life's decisions is 100% the correct thing to do. Every important matter that I first bathed in prayer brought God's assurance and a good outcome. But at other times, my decisions failed because I let human factors like pride and selfishness get in the way. As a result, mistakes were made including the one that landed me in prison with a 13½ to 27-year sentence. Oh, how much different it would have been if I had done it God's way instead of mine.

Dancing With The Devil

CHAPTER TWENTY

PAPERS NOW SERVED

Here's how things unfolded. I had dodged the deputy for so long that I was getting a little crazy. Even when he hadn't been spotted approaching the job I'd get all jumpy just expecting him. My nerves were shot.

Furthermore, when things went wrong on the job, I'd throw a running fit. If I couldn't get my measurements right, I'd throw my tools out the window and kick material around. And I would often leave the site in a panicked frenzy.

You know, I was rough on people and I was hard to put up with, but I had some great carpenters working with me. Thankfully--years later when I returned home--they were all still my friends. In the end, they still cared about me and that meant a lot.

So how did the divorce come about? And how did the deputy finally catch me? Well, I grew so tired of avoiding those papers I finally gave in to the inevitable and turned myself in to the Sheriff. I said, "Hey Randy, I guess you have something to give me, don't you?"

He handed me a big brown envelope with the divorce documents inside. I just gave up and signed them. That's when it hit me like a ton of bricks. We were getting a divorce.

STORIES

A few days later, I started selling off our household furniture. I sold our piano, the living room set, and a yellow roll-top desk and chair that Nora was very attached to. (I probably did it subconsciously just to hurt her.)

100

I sort of had a plan too. I thought I would at some point take the balance of Nora's belongings to her, in Pittsburgh, and then skip the country. I had a friend in Kitchener, Ontario, Canada. I figured I'd go there for a visit and see if maybe the situation would cool down. It might not have been the best idea, but it was all I had, so I stuck to the plan.

It was a depressing time and I cared less and less about everything. I continually tried to contact Nora in Pittsburgh but she made that virtually impossible. I was sure she was getting in deeper with her family and that they were filling her head with stories, persuading her to stay put and leave me behind. She was probably giving them an earful too, exaggerating and making up things to tell them in order to avoid telling the truth about her adulterous lifestyle.

They had to be influencing her about what she should do and she was probably buying into their advice. This kind of thing is like a small forest fire. At first, it's barely noticeable; then it begins to feed on itself; before long it gets completely out of control. This situation was definitely raging out of control but it was the children and me who were the ones being burned.

NORA PLAYS THE VICTIM CARD

The next thing I heard was that Nora went to live in a "battered women's shelter". I guess she was determined to paint a bad picture of me. She drummed up some story about how I had physically abused her, while the truth is, in our years of marriage, I never once hit her or caused any harm to come to her; quite the opposite was true. I was caring and attentive to her wants and needs, perhaps overly so. But I'm sure this was only one of many sparks that lit the fire, now wildly burning.

I will say this: the emotional pain I endured brought out the worst in me. I acted in ways I didn't want to and I wasn't as kind as I could have been. I had to keep my guard up because I never knew what was coming next. Pain caused by a broken heart can attack a person in so many ways. The rejection alone was so bad it was surreal. It was like a dream. I found myself running to get away and getting nowhere.

I wasn't acting much like the new man God wanted me to be. I had actually turned into that old flesh-man I used to be. I should have held on to my faith; my virtues should have served as a good witness. Instead, I really let the Lord down. When I saw my life flitting away before my eyes, I felt helpless and overwhelmed by my own faulty understanding. And the one person I needed to turn to--my mate and partner--had now become my enemy. It forced me into a world of *me and mine, tit for tat*, and *hurt me and I'll hurt you back,* so-to-speak.

AMANDA AND HOPE

My only remaining joy came from my children and I loved them more than life. Now, every shred of energy I had was focused on them and I decided that even if I couldn't have my wife, I would not lose my children. They had never hurt me, they had always accepted the love I had for them, and I would lay my life down for them any time, for any reason. Little did I know, that time was coming soon.

So in my head, I had established that first of all, the kids were mine, and secondly, I wanted their family to be put back together again. They deserved a normal life; after all, they had done nothing wrong and should be cared for and protected by a mother and a father.

I prayed and hoped and prayed some more when, miraculously, I heard from Nora. We talked things over by phone and made the decision that if I would give up and sell out my business and bring all our belongings to Pittsburgh, we would begin again. We would start over and rebuild our family like it was supposed to be.

So that's exactly what I did. I rented a U-Haul truck and a tow dolly for the car and when it was all loaded I headed for Pittsburgh. I wasn't happy to be leaving Georgia to move North but if that's what it took to save my marriage and our household, then I was all for it.

EYES WIDE OPEN

I went to Pittsburgh as previously planned, and the kids were glad to see me as usual. When we finished greeting each other, I sat with them in the kitchen for a few moments.

All I can tell you is what I saw with my own eyes. I certainly wouldn't want to make false accusations or anything, but I became very suspicious of some things, and here's why:

Nora was sitting at the table with two girlfriends, and the kids were darting all over the place. As we sat and made small talk I noticed a very distinguished ring on one of Nora's girlfriend's left hand. Then, to my amazement, I saw the very same ring on Nora's finger. The girlfriend quickly shifted her hands under the table, all the while trying to be nonchalant. My poker face was perfect. I kept right on talking like I hadn't noticed a thing. In a few moments, her hands were back in plain sight, but the ring was gone. I guess she must have put it in her pocket.

WHAT?

The small-talk ended and I started unloading the furniture from the truck, all the while still figuring I could be wrong. I talked myself into feeling better, thinking we were going to be a whole family again! I was so encouraged in the moment.

What I didn't know was that Nora and her girlfriends were carrying all *my* belongings to the front porch as fast as I could unload them. When it was time for me to take the U-Haul back Nora told me where my stuff was and that I needed to go and load it back up. With laughter ringing in her voice, she said, "I guess I fooled you, didn't I?"

"What?" I heard myself say in disbelief. I was not only shocked but infuriated. She had done it to me a second time: once by her leaving under the pretense that her father needed brain surgery, and now again by drawing me here under false hopes. I vowed this would be the last time.

We exchanged a few meaningless words while the kids kept asking to go for a ride. So I thought it might be good to take them out for a while. I wanted some time with them anyway, before heading back to Georgia. Since my car was still attached to the U-Haul, everyone agreed I should take them with me to return it. We could go to the mall after that for some serious ice cream and chit chat.

We sat down with our cones and my oldest daughter who was six, began to tell me about mommy's new girlfriend. She explained that one day she walked into mommy's room and saw them in bed together, kissing, just like her and daddy used to do. She didn't understand what that was about and she was looking to me for answers.

I don't know what I said, but I muddled through some kind of an explanation. Mostly, I comforted her because there was no way to explain such facts to a six-year-old. In my mind, of course, I had it all figured out and the story matched another one I had heard through a friend who knew them both. I realized my daughters were living in a very detrimental situation and I knew if I were to leave them now, I'd be very sorry for how their lives would turn out. I may never have a life with them as their daddy again.

CHAPTER TWENTY-ONE

NORTHBOUND AFTER ALL!

Instead of taking the girls back to Nora's place, I took off with them to Canada. At least I'd be able to salvage *some* happiness. And, perhaps selfishly, I knew keeping them was the winning shot against Nora, to pay her back for hurting me. Since she was so competitive, this last blow was poetically perfect. Yes, that's an absolutely horrible way for a Christian to be thinking and nothing could have been farther from Christ's example. But there it is: mankind is utterly depraved when he shuts God out, isn't he?

So I went North after all, with the children, that is. We left Pittsburgh and three hundred miles later, we landed in Toronto, Canada. Surprisingly, the girls and I really loved it there. We were having such a wonderful time of closeness that I didn't want it to end. Things were better for us up there than they had been in months.

I was thinking too, that I was buying some time with Nora, and that we might be able to talk and put a stop to the divorce. Even though the papers had been filed, I still wanted to save our marriage. Now that I was safely in Canada, I thought I could call Nora and have her come up for a while. Maybe if she would get away from the other influences in her life, we could have a fair chance at working out our problems. I was crazy enough to believe it could work.

You see, I had taken a very serious vow before God: marriage was forever. I wasn't playing around; no joking here; we were married for keeps. Now I wanted to do something . . . anything . . . to get it back.

I called Nora to let her know where we were and that we were O.K. After some discussion, she said she would come up and visit. I thought we were really making some strides toward reconciliation. We would try to figure out what we needed to do to start over again. And maybe things could be even better than before! I had so much hope, but I was so blind.

I wanted to trust Nora. This woman had been my wife and I still believed in her. Well, the operative phrase here is: *had been*. And if you suspect any bitterness in my voice, you are correct. I was about to get my fill of this bitter cup. It was full and running over, and I wasn't prepared for it at all. My blind faith in her promises tricked me once again.

THE LAW, AND THE PHILOSOPHY OF
MARRIAGE AND DIVORCE

I can see now that before leaving for Canada, I had other options, but I had thrown my good sense to the wind. Rejection had marred my capacity to think straight. Soon, by law, everything important to me would be taken away and I wished I had an emergency quick-fix. After all, this was *my* marriage and *my* family. But by the simple, swift stroke of a judges pen, my wife and children would be gone. I knew my plan would make it hard to undo this kind of damage, once done, but I was about to go ahead with it anyway.

My dad used to say, "If you go to the top of the Empire State Building and break open a feather pillow, you can never go back down and pick up all the feathers." I could plainly see that some of the feathers we had scattered would be irretrievable; lost in the winds of deceit; the damage would be irreversible.

It's just the same when a person hurries along to get a divorce. It can be impossible for one to find their way back from that. The doors of opportunity close, and there's no second chance to take another look. I was trying to hold that door open but others were pushing hard to force it closed.

Divorce situations need a cooling off period. Consequences should be considered more intently. But instead, a judge signs a divorce decree as if it were a part of his daily routine, and that's it. It's forgotten and *little ones* are hurt in the process. The innocent are destroyed because the guilty one is the mouthpiece that gets all the attention. The judgment becomes fatally final.

I knew that with one indifferent signature by a judge, our lives could virtually be wiped out. To me, that was deplorable. How *dare* he? He had no interest in our lives. He had no real knowledge regarding how this judgment would affect us. We need laws in this world, but the letter of the law should always protect the innocent.

I want to get on my soapbox here: how in the world can a judge minister fairness without seeing the whole picture? How can he be so insensitive as to treat these cases as routine? How is it that he's not personally touched by these situations anymore? Well, I guess that's another topic for another day.

So I knew I was facing a divorce I didn't want. I was grasping at straws, looking for solutions to my marital problems. Little did I know, I would face even more suffering ahead in this learning process God had me in.

FOOLED ME ONCE

There's an old expression in the South: "Fool me once, shame on you; fool me twice, shame on me."

Well, I was fooled not once or twice, but *several* times by my wife! So shame, shame, shame on me.

I was easy to fool, I suppose, because I was so focused on keeping my family intact. I heard just what I wanted to hear. All the while, Nora wasn't anybody's fool. She knew just how to take full advantage of me.

During her visit, we talked about many things. I thought we had reached at least a few working agreements. That's why I let her take the children back with her to Pittsburgh, while I finished the job I had started in Canada. (I was helping build a restaurant.)

We said our goodbyes and got to the part where they were leaving me to go down the highway. I got a big knot in my stomach. I heard a warning cry in my spirit that said, "Doug, you're making a mistake." So I got in my car and quickly caught up with them. I motioned them to stop and we all pulled over to the side of the road. Everybody got out.

I came up with the lame excuse that I wanted to kiss the kids goodbye one more time. But *really*, I wanted to see how Nora would react to my stopping her. I just couldn't get over this feeling that things weren't right; that things were not as they seemed. At the same time, I felt a little foolish. Nora had pulled over and stopped so easily. Surely, everything was fine.

I kissed the children and said goodbye again. I told them I would see them in a few weeks. They climbed back in the car and set out en-route, but the troubled feeling I had wouldn't go away. I followed them down the highway awhile longer, but I couldn't stop them every few miles. So I finally turned back to Toronto to complete my work assignment.

I spent two more weeks in Ontario, finishing things up. Then I headed back to Pittsburgh. I called Nora along the way and she suggested we meet at a place called Elby's Restaurant. We both thought it would be neutral ground and a good place to hopefully work on plans to reconcile.

I arrived at the appointed place at the appointed time. I parked my car across the street where it was sort of hidden from plain view. I went inside and Nora and the kids were there, waiting for me. Our greeting was cordial. I sat down and we started talking.

After a few pleasantries, we got to the heart of the matter. But it didn't take me long to become disappointed. Nora made it quite clear that she was not going to keep our previous agreements. I wasn't surprised though. But I was hurt that she just couldn't keep her word. She failed to let her "yea be yea and her nay be nay", (so the Bible says).

I grew up when men shook hands and didn't worry about written contracts. A man's word was enough, and that was always good enough for me. In those days, people stood by their agreements. I expected the same, here. It should have been really simple but as I said, those were the good old days. Now here I was in a shame-on-me situation, once again.

CHAPTER TWENTY-TWO

ON THE ROAD AGAIN

When I realized that my home life wasn't going to be restored, I knew I'd have to muster up the courage for plan "B". You see, I had mistrusted Nora; I figured she would probably dupe me again. Furthermore, I didn't trust her with my children and I didn't want them living in that disgraceful environment any longer. So yes, I had a plan "B" in place, but I wasn't exactly proud of it.

As we left the restaurant and crossed the street, my head was racing. Then, in the blink of an eye, I made my move. I suddenly swept up the kids--one in each arm--and ran for the car where I actually had a friend waiting. It was a *play* I had taken out of his playbook! He was crouched down behind the steering wheel and as I dove into the back seat with the kids, he started the car and we took off.

My heart was beating with indescribable fear, but at least I had my children, and possibly the leverage I needed to still work out a reconciliation. I know, I know. I was going about it all wrong. But it's not possible to live in another person's shoes. I did my best even though my actions were amiss.

If I had waited patiently on the Lord, things may have worked out differently, but I did what I had to do because I didn't want to be tricked anymore. Worst-case scenario: even if the marriage ended, at least I'd have my kids. I loved them and they loved me, so back to Canada we went.

I WAS SO TIRED

This time we avoided the Peace Bridge at Niagara and went by way of Detroit because Nora was smart enough to have probably had the Niagara route under surveillance. We arrived at the Canadian border but had a harder time getting across. They wanted our birth certificates so we were detained for about half an hour. In the end, the holdup was really because they wanted papers on the fellow I was riding with. He was wanted in Pittsburgh so they kept him and refused entry for me. Now, what was I to do?

After being turned away at the Detroit/Windsor border crossing, we headed back to Detroit. We mulled around there for a few hours and then I started feeling bad. I regretted my poor decision and thought maybe Nora had enough of a scare this time and wouldn't pull any more tricks.

If I came back, maybe now we could sit down and talk about saving our family. Maybe now she would be honest with me and bridges could be mended. I knew the farther I ran, the more destructive it would be to that goal. If she would accept my apologies and was willing to work things out, I was ready.

I was tired of running, tired of the secrecies, tired of the pressures on the children, tired of seeing us get nowhere. If only I had sought God and put His wisdom to work, things would have been so much better. But I was hard headed and I wasn't in the habit of going to the Lord for advice, so I carried on alone and stumbled over every decision I made.

I needed to get my mind off of this mess, so the kids and I went bowling. The girls were four and six years old and had never bowled before. Amanda, my oldest girl, got a strike for the very first time in her life! She squealed with glee and it was music to my ears. We all had a lot of fun. That night became a special memory for me, and it was one of the few comforts I clung to later on when I was in prison.

When we finished our game, we used the payphone in the bowling alley so the kids could call their Mom. Even though I'd made mistakes, I still had enough consideration to keep Nora informed of where we were and how the girls were. That's a lot more than she had done for me but I felt it was the right thing to do. If I hadn't loved her I wouldn't have bothered, but real love lasts through thick and thin. I had to do what was right, whether I was tired or not.

When we were done talking I found us a motel for the night and took advantage of some much-needed sleep. It had been a long, long day.

MY LOST CHILD FROM DAYS PAST

I should have been wiser. I should have realized how cruel Nora was. You see, when *she* took the kids and left me in Georgia it was like she had disappeared off of the face of the earth. She didn't call *me* to let me know they were alright. I never knew where they were or how they were doing. She must have realized how devastated I would be.

When she vanished from Toccoa with our kids, she had to know it was the hardest blow she could have given me, and she probably enjoyed it. My nerves were shot and I almost went crazy. For four months I laid on our living room floor and cried. When I was all cried out there was still no comfort to be had. When I tried to pray, I came up empty. The pain was so great I thought my head would burst open at the seams.

My wife knew that years earlier I had a daughter sold into an illegal adoption. For twenty years and a month, I lived with the pain of not knowing if she was dead or alive. I suffered through the horrors of losing my first daughter. I told Nora how I felt about it, often, and I couldn't believe she had tormented me all over again.

It was only by the grace of God that I had any forgiveness or compassion left for her. Although she had "done it unto me", in time, I learned to not "do it unto her". That's why I called her from the road to ease her mind. It was the right thing to do. But how could I bring myself to consider her? It was only through the power of God that I was able to stay on the right track. In my flesh, I didn't want to be nice to her at all.

FOOLED ME TWICE (SHAME, SHAME)

Have I mentioned that I loved my children?! That was the bottom line for me. I was prepared to do anything for them, but there were obstacles. For one thing, I was stuck in Detroit, on the run with my kids, and I had nowhere to go. Canada had turned me away and I didn't have a plan "C". I guess I could have gone to my family in Illinois, but I figured that area would be covered by watchful police, so that was not an option.

I was loaded up with mixed emotions and running out of ideas. I believed taking my kids was in their best interest, but at the same time, I wanted to reconcile with my wife. Now we were hundreds of miles apart, and this whole thing was working overtime in my head. What else could I do but give her another call?

The phone rang a couple of times before she picked it up. She acted surprised to hear from me but we talked and everything seemed cool. Some tentative agreements were made yet again. She spoke to the kids and made promises about putting our family back together. (I can't forgive her for lying to them.) Yes, this was exactly what the girls had been asking for, and it was what I wanted to hear too. With that being said I headed home.

Our spirits were running high and we enjoyed eating supper and bedding down for the night, anticipating good things for the day ahead. In the morning we called Nora and left out for Pittsburgh. We sang songs along the way and joy rose up inside of us. We couldn't seem to drive fast enough to get there!

Nora had mentioned she wanted us to stop and call her at a set time because she wanted to have everything *arranged*. (Little did I know what she meant by that.) When I stopped to call her, she gave me another stopping point to call from. Following that, she asked me to call again in an hour, just to let her know where we were. I thought, "Gee, she's actually excited about our coming back. That's great news. All's well that ends well!" I believed everything was going to be O.K. I was choked up with gladness and I couldn't see beyond it.

We agreed to meet each other in Youngstown, Ohio. That way she could see us sooner and we could make an outing of it, as a family. I liked that idea. It might be nice to have our new beginnings just across the border from Pittsburgh. Pittsburgh reminded me of hurt, lies, and failures.

The last time I called her she said she'd be late because of a flat tire. She had to get it changed so she gave me a contact number to call her. Of course, I forgot I had just put a brand new set of tires on her car, so, blindly I listened to her story and felt sorry that she was having so much trouble.

Then I thought, "I'm wasting time here. I could drive further and meet her somewhere else." I suggested that to her and she agreed. She asked me to meet at exit two on highway seventy-six. That would give her time to get the tire fixed. Then we could meet and have lunch together.

Great. I agreed. She told me there was a gas station/convenience store at that location and there was a payphone on the corner. I could call her again to make sure she was there, and if she was a bit late, I could just park and wait for her. But we should be together within the hour!

CHAPTER TWENTY-THREE

BUSTED

Yes, yes, yes! The kids and I were so happy. We drove another 40 miles and turned right, off of exit number two. Just down the road a bit was the convenience store, and the telephone booth was on the corner. It was as easy as pie.

I parked near the pay-phone and fished out some quarters. I dialed the number, and Nora answered. I was surprised! I wasn't expecting her to answer because she was supposed to be on her way. Never-the-less, I was as glad as could be and said, "Hi, honey. We're here, waiting for you. When will you get here?"

The rest of the conversation was never clear in my mind. Thinking back, I do remember saying, "My God, Nora! There are cop cars all over the place out here. What? . . . Uh, wait a minute! . . . They're getting out and . . . my God, they've got guns and everything! They're pointing them at me! Nora . . . what's going on? I don't get it . . . Nora, have *you* done this? Have you done this to us?! Oh - - my - - God . . . "

THE RIDE DOWNTOWN

So the final card was played. I had been tricked, kicked in the gut, and captured with no way out. The officers approached me very carefully, demanding I keep my hands in sight.

They handcuffed and shackled me right in front of my girls; my poor little girls. They were crying and clutching my pant legs saying, "Please, please don't hurt my daddy. Please don't take him away from us."

The arresting officers could see they weren't going to pry them from me, so they let us all ride together in the back seat of the squad car.

When we got to the state police station, the handcuffs were removed but the shackles remained. The temperature must have been in the nineties and the girls were hot and needed attention. The processing officer allowed me to go to my car, which had been towed in behind us, to get a hairbrush and toothbrushes for the girls.

While I was brushing their hair and putting up braids and ponytails, the officer who was taking down the information on me kept looking at me over the top of his glasses. He tried to keep his head down in his paperwork, but he hadn't fooled me for a second. I knew he was watching me like a hawk. Maybe he thought I'd try to run. Little did he know, I'd rather die than leave my children behind. Although he was suspicious of me, I still thought he was likable.

At some point, he lay his pen down with a very definite motion and turned to me: "Mr. Veer, is your wife an attorney?"

I said, "No."

Then he continued, "Mr. Veer, there's something very wrong here."

That's all I needed to hear. More accusations from a complete stranger at that. I replied, "What's that?"

"Well, I can't tell you what's in this report, exactly, but . . . you really do love those kids, don't you?"

Surprised by his statement I said, "Of course I do! Do you think I'd be wrapped up in all this foolishness if I didn't?"

After a long pause, he said, "That's exactly what I'm talking about. It just doesn't fit together. You're more concerned over your children's needs than with what's happening to you. No, it just doesn't make sense."

GETTING THE SCOOP

I couldn't help wonder why they had shackled me. I wasn't a murderer or anything. Then the arresting officer revealed parts of the situation to me from what you might call the prosecutor's point of view.

"You should have seen how your wife described you," he explained. "She told us to be afraid of you. She said you'd have a big knife strapped to your side, and she motioned with her hands, from her hip to her knee. You know. Something like Crocodile Dundee. She dabbed her eyes with a tissue when she talked about her fear of you. It bothered me at the time because I couldn't see any tears. Even so, she insisted that we please be careful because you'd probably come out *shootin'!*"

I was shocked, to say the least. I hadn't owned a gun since I was twelve years old. I used to have a little single shot "22". And I've never carried a knife. I always figured a real man didn't have to; especially a man who trusted God and moved in circles far removed from dangerous elements and crazy people.

Then the cop asked if I was sure my wife wasn't an attorney. I told him she wasn't. He went on to say that Nora had everything laid out the way an attorney would have done, and she talked the way an attorney would talked. That led me to the sinking realization that this whole trip was a setup, and was well orchestrated by someone who had helped her.

Later on, I learned through another officer that every telephone call I made was being recorded by the

F.B.I. on a tapped line, authorized by her. I was indeed fooled by Nora for the third time.

THE REALITY OF BEING ARRESTED

When Nora and I had met at Elby's in West Virginia, I never dreamed that as a father not yet divorced from his wife, I could be charged with kidnaping my own children. All I was trying to do was prevent a divorce or a permanent separation. I was always duty bound to do *anything* to protect my family as a husband and dad. Who would have thought this could happen to someone in America?

When I went through the dam break at Toccoa Falls in 1977, I was willing to give up my life that night to save my family. Now, eight years later, I was in just as much of a crisis. To *do* or to *die* was my ultimate responsibility. That's why, during my preliminary hearings in two different states, I didn't try to hide my actions. I did not deny what I had done.

Had I tried, I'm sure some hot shot lawyer would have helped me cover up my deeds, and I could have gotten off. But my being a Christian required honesty, even in the toughest of circumstances. I needed to get up every morning and face that God-mirror even before I looked at my own face. God reflects His Spirit back toward us and shows us who we really are. I had to keep that relationship pure, and telling the truth was part of it.

If I had lied, I would have had to face the Lord every second of every morning, noon, and night, explaining why I hadn't trusted Him as my attorney and my advocate. Oh, how happy I am that when I finally faced the music, God cleared my guilty conscience. I stood up for my principles. Yes, I admitted I had broken the law, but my motives were true. In my heart, I was just protecting my children. In turn, God protected me as His child, even as I was taken into federal custody.

At my hearing, the judge asked me no less than three times: if I had it to do over again, wouldn't I have done it differently. Each time my answer was "No." I told him that after what I saw; that is, the lifestyle being lived in my wife's home, I felt compelled to take my children away and I wasn't sorry for it. Three times he tried to help me but I would have had to lie, so three times I turned down his extremely gracious offer. He had no recourse but to hold me over for trial. Even so, I've never been sorry that I refused his help.

CHAPTER TWENTY-FOUR

THE CELL DOOR

The door to the cell block slammed shut and locked me in. I was on the other side of freedom, and the mocking echo of the prison door rang in my ears. Reality had struck me. Reality was here. It was up close and in my face. Honestly, I believed I'd never experience freedom again. I expected to draw my very last breath, right here; here in this cold, dirty Hell-hole.

I stood, staring at the crusty old bars. I was alone and afraid. I so much wanted to embrace my disbelief. But my gut-wrenching disgust overwhelmed me.

"God, where are you?" I whispered. "Are You in here? . . . Please help me."

The facts washed over me. I thought, "This is real. I've been arrested." I wanted to scream, "My God! How could this be true? How could this be possible?" But only silence filled the jail cell. Dreadful, ugly silence.

THE ARRESTING OFFICER

Let me go back a bit and tell you more about the arresting officer. Two hours after my arrest, this same officer went with me to the Magistrate Judge to have my bond set. He told the judge that from what he saw and how I had interacted with my girls, the statements reported by my wife might not have been exactly truthful. He actually pleaded before the judge for me! He said that under the circumstances, I should be given some leeway until this went to trial. He asked that I be given an O.R. which means to be released in my own recognizance.

Well, the judge must have thought this cop was absolutely crazy to go to bat for a bearded, rough-looking individual like me. In spite of his proposition, the judge said, "Yes, I'll see that he has a chance for bail. I am setting it at $135,000, cash only. Get him out of here!" Needless to say, the officer stood there in shock.

Later, I learned that I was considered violent and was nicknamed, "Rambo", due to Nora's descriptive complaint against me. Of course, that's what the judge was focused on, but my arresting officer didn't buy it. The fact is, he gave me his personal card and told me if he could ever do anything for me to please contact him. And he wanted me to look him up when it was all over to let him know how things turned out.

I carried that little yellow card around for about four years and I never forgot what a nice person he was. I've often wondered if he was a Christian. One day I'd like to look him up and thank him and find out where his life is with Christ.

There were other policemen at the scene, but they weren't as kind. For example, when Nora showed up at the "crime scene", the cops let her open the trunk, go through my car, and take anything she wanted. As a result, I wound up losing many things that were important to me: photo albums with pictures of my past, my kids, and other personal belongings.

Here's a little footnote about being caught on the other side of freedom. One minute you're a "class A" citizen. The next minute you're treated like human refuse; like the worst misfit on the planet. (Of course, I'm talking about the average, everyday citizen. A person with a political standing does *not* get this kind of treatment. They're housed in a sleek, country club atmosphere while serving out their time.)

Through this experience, I developed a real appreciation for the Apostle Paul. He suffered in prison undeservedly. The journals of history contain many other stories of suffering saints who gave of themselves for the sake of spreading the Gospel. Without these martyrs, we wouldn't have the freedom to worship as we do today.

Yes, we take far too much for granted. These iron bars were just the beginning of my appreciation for freedom. This *other side of freedom* was as foreign to me as Greek, but learning about the lack of freedom was about to become stamped into my memory forever.

THE ARRAIGNMENT

After sitting in a cell for a few days, the next major step was my arraignment. For those unfamiliar with this word, it means pretrial or preliminary court hearing whereby charges are formally brought against the defendant in the presence of his accuser. This is where I would enter a plea of guilty or not guilty. Then a judge would decide whether a trial would follow or whether the charges should be dropped.

I thought I would finally be able to tell *my* side of the story. I believed the presiding magistrate would intelligently and impartially decide this case and deem it to be not worthy of a trial. The truth is, it was the closest thing to a kangaroo court I had ever seen. And yes, it was decided that there would be a trial.

Nora sat there like a poor, pathetic child telling her story. I, by this time, looked very unkept, rough, and dirty. And the handcuffs gave me the appearance of a real hardened criminal or a psycho. Needless to say, I was treated like one.

When my time came, I wasn't allowed to say much at all. The court seemed to be biased against me. Every question fired at me came directly out of Nora's list of accusations. And each of her statements had just enough truth to bring out the worst impression of me.

Furthermore, the pretrial should have taken place within 72 hours of my arrest. The law states that after 72 hours I should have been released. But my rights were violated. Almost a week had passed before my arraignment came. And I repeat: the bond was cash only in the amount of $135,000 dollars. Good luck with that!

With all this working against me, I would have been better off not going to the arraignment. When it was over, I remember going back to my cell and writing the following statement in the front leaf of my Bible: "Friday, September 13th, I went to the preliminary hearing and sat across from Nora. Dear God . . . teach me about love!"

Here was a wife with whom I had spent over ten years. We had three children together and now she was seated across from me in a court of law, not as a helpmate but as an adversary. In my "flower child days", I thought love meant "never having to say you're sorry". You know: let bygones be bygones. It used to sound so good. But this thing called love now puzzled me. All I could think to say was, "What's it all about, Alfie?"

I should mention, too, that my wedding anniversary was the very next day, September 14th, 1985, but the old fires of my youth had now become ashes of sorrow.

CHOOSING GOD IN THE FACE OF THE TEMPTER

I was becoming keenly aware of how serious this thing was. And as I got to know other inmates, my eyes were opened to their ways of doing things. There were scores of guys around with *experience* in these matters. I even found lawyers behind these same bars who sat down and helped me construct a detailed analysis of my situation. Yes, I was offered all kinds of *help* to deal with my wife.

At first, their ideas sounded good. I wanted to get a plan going against her. After all, my being here was her fault, and boy was I angry about it! My hatred was hot enough to burn down a stone wall. I felt so righteous; I was above reproach, I thought. How could she dare do this to me? I did what was right and then she had me arrested for it!

My fellow inmates suggested I *plant a little evidence* to get her in trouble. I could arrange to have some drugs put in her car, to sort of help things along; something that would get her locked up. Maybe she could even *disappear* if you know what I mean. The sky was the limit, really, and these guys were on my side. They could get the job done, even though she was on the outside and I wasn't.

I pondered it all in my spirit but came to realize I had to refuse such help. How could I walk the Christian walk, or be the *jailhouse preacher man* when in my heart I wanted revenge against my wife? So I dropped the whole thing and chose to obey the Lord. I was through taking matters into my own hands. Instead, I trusted God, believing He would work it all out for me. I stood on the Scripture that said I was one of His children, and that I was the **". . . called, according to His purpose . . ."** (Romans 8:28).

DETERMINED

With that in mind, I made a determination. I promised the Lord I would not hate Nora, nor would I become bitter. Instead, I would call upon His great strength to help me find a respectable, God-honoring way out of my situation. In my Bible that I had with me, I wrote down my commitment and from that moment on I walked in forgiveness toward Nora. Not just for her crimes against me, but even for what she was yet to do against me and my children.

I firmly believe that right then, God stepped in and took full control of me and my entire future. I praise Him because of His wonderful love. I found my way back to *the other (right) side of freedom*. I had peace in my soul and I wasn't bitter. I was obedient and not vengeful. I was forgiving and not hateful.

So many inmates carry destructive emotions and therefore have a hard time adjusting to the outside world when the time comes. Bitterness can really eat away at a person's peace of mind; even one's guts become torn up. I never did have to deal with that. Praise God!

CHAPTER TWENTY-FIVE

WALKING BY FAITH

My arraignment came and went, and the time of my trial drew nearer. I knew the only *real* tool at my disposal was prayer. I had *talked the talk* of a Christian man. Now I'd have to *walk the walk* so the world could see how true it was. Could I really live by faith and not by sight?

Thinking back, I had many good years of teaching, especially from Dad Ronson. I learned so much from him, and from other godly people, too. There were plenty of living examples to emulate. Now it was time to show whether I was just playing with God or if I really meant business.

WHAT IS FREEDOM?

There's a saying in this great country of ours that's supposed to build confidence into the very fabric of who we are. It is said that "a man is innocent until he is proven guilty". I say, "what a laugh!" I always thought the statement was true and that justice was on our side. Then the judicial system caught me in its web of legalism.

Instead, the declaration should be revised: "Unless and until a man can hire a few good lawyers to prove he is innocent, a man is guilty from the very beginning!"

This is the truth about our wonderful system. Don't get me wrong. I still believe America is the finest country in the world and I wouldn't trade her for anything. But through the years, the concept of having to prove one's guilt has been lost.

Let me give you an example. Let's say I go to a magistrate and claim that you beat me, took my billfold, and threatened to beat me again with a baseball bat. Based on my word, you would be arrested. I would simply sign a document containing the above accusation, it would be co-signed by a judge, and you would be sent to jail. You'd stay there until you could either come up with the required bond or until your hearing was scheduled.

Now let's say your bail was set at $2000. You'd have to come up with ten percent of that or $200, and give it to the bail bondsman. That little fee would never be returned to you, regardless of the outcome. The fee is paid to the bondsman for his risk that you could run before your hearing. (And if you run, the bondsman pays the whole $2000.) Now, if you can't get a bond arranged, you could end up sitting in jail for six months or longer, just waiting for your trial.

If I argue convincingly enough that you really did violate me, you may even be sentenced for it! But if somehow, you manage to prove that I'm the liar (which would be extremely hard to do), you could only rectify the injustice by spending more time and money on attorneys to prove your case. And that my friend is the justice system today.

Does it seem unbelievably absurd to you? Well, that's just the tip of the iceberg if *you're* the one behind bars. Once you're there, you're branded as guilty and treated accordingly, and you're considered a criminal for practically the rest of your life. Yes, my friend, this is the law today. You are guilty until proven innocent.

Mark Twain once said that the two most wonderful words in the English language are "not guilty". I've wondered if he learned that because of a run-in with the law. After my release, I'd sometimes sit and reason with myself when things got a little tough. I'd console myself by admitting, "it's O.K. there's still nothing better than freedom." I meant it then and I still mean it today.

TRANSFERRED TO ANOTHER FACILITY

So I was arraigned and then transferred from Beaver Falls, Pennsylvania to Pittsburgh. They transported me in handcuffs and shackles which was traumatic for me. I was actually going to be incarcerated and it really hit home. Here I was in a major holding facility awaiting federal trial for several charges. It was more than my mind could comprehend.

I felt like an outsider looking in. It was like watching my life on T.V. or something. I thought I could wake myself up and it would all be over. Slowly, it began to sink in: "Doug Veer, this is your life."

I prayed, "Lord, can't you stop this train and let me off?" Nothing but pending doom lay ahead. I've always been quite perceptive, but this time I wished I was wrong about what would happen next.

When we got to Pittsburgh, I walked up to those foreboding stairs. I felt like I was about to walk the plank or that proverbial last mile. For many a man, that's exactly what this walk was.

Once inside the building, I was given an extremely humiliating strip search including an examination of my private parts. Then I was unshackled and put in the *bullpen*. This is where multiple numbers of other convicts are held for processing.

We were *processed* all right. It reminded me of the chicken plants back home in Northeast Georgia. That's where many a chicken would suffer a humiliating death. Each one was tied up by its feet, like me. And stripped naked, like me. And probed and felt all over, like me. And finally, neatly packed and tucked away, never to be thought of again, just like me. Yup. Assembly line justice. Unexamined. Impersonal. Uncaring. It was just another day at the slaughterhouse.

MY PRISON NAME--LET IT BEGIN

This different dimension I had stepped into was like the *Twilight Zone.* Soon, even my name would be forgotten.

People don't think about what's in a name. My first name was given to me by my Mother because of her love for her brother, Ralph Dyson. My Mother chose my middle name because of the great character of General Douglas MacArthur. So officially, I'm Ralph Douglas Veer, but I came to use my middle name, Doug. It just worked better for me. Now, my name was replaced by a number, and I was lost in the inescapable vastness of the prison system.

I don't remember all the details but my family filled in the gaps later. I do remember thinking back to Harlem Elementary School and seeing my name on my sixth-grade report card, next to a whole bunch of "A"s. I wanted to show it to everyone. Imagine a grade sheet filled with honors and my name at the top! That was true happiness for a twelve-year-old kid. Wow!

Five years later my name was displayed once again with beautifully handwritten silver scrolling on an oval walnut plaque. In the center of the plaque was a large gold plated insignia for submarine service. I had just graduated from submarine school in New London, Connecticut and I was given this plaque with distinguished honors for having been in the top third of my graduating class with a 94.6 average. At 17 years of age, I had a real sense of pride and accomplishment over that.

Now, here I was many years later. My name was displayed once again. It was written in full so there would be no mistake about it:

NAME: Ralph Douglas Veer
CHARGE: Kidnapping/Assault/Aggravated Felony 3
SENTENCE: 13½ to 27 years

So where was the happiness now? Where was the pride? Had sin finally taken its toll?

Proverbs 16:18 says, **"Pride goeth before destruction, and an haughty spirit before a fall."** The chapter goes on to talk about the virtues of the humble: **"Better it is to be of an humble spirit with the lowly, than to divide the spoil with the proud,"** (verse 19).

If only I could have heeded that verse. If only I saw that there wouldn't be any worthwhile spoil to divide in this place. It was just a cold, lonely prison where I would spend hours, days, weeks, months, and years and years and years.

The prison had been built in 1883. Then in 1977, it was given a facelift and restored. They modernized it as well, adding automatic doors and an updated infirmary.

Inside it was 91 feet high, with rows of cells piled one on top of the other. On the higher outside walls was a great bridge reaching across the street to another building where there were court-rooms and official offices. The great archway connecting the buildings was very appropriately called "The Bridge of Sighs". It was named for the many men who walked across it with heavy hearts knowing they would face a judge for sentencing. Soon, it would be my turn to make that long walk.

Suddenly, I was roused from my musings. I heard the cell door's loud "Claaang-g-g!". It had the fury of a freight train. It passed within inches of my face as it continued to drag in its tracks: "Claaang-g-g!" The echo traveled along the corridor and joined in the chorus of subsequent doors sliding and slamming shut, one after the next. The range vibrated and the mocking song rang out, "for everrr . . . " I listened until the echo faded into a whisper and finally disappeared into the long, dark night.

CHAPTER TWENTY-SIX

THE SHRINK WAS CRAZY!

My incarceration began in 1985 and I served my time in three different prisons: Allegheny County, (Pennsylvania), Clearfield County which we called "Cornfield" County, and Brooke County, (West Virginia). I was up for three varying charges of kidnapping, interference with custody of children, assault, and theft by unlawful taking. My resulting convictions carried a minimum sentence of 13½ years and a maximum of 27 years, so it was very possible that I would spend the rest of my life behind bars and die there.

When I first arrived at Allegheny, I went through an indoctrination period which took several days. It was a radical change of lifestyle and the exercise was supposed to help me get used to the place. (Like really: would anyone ever get used to it?) This time period also gave the officials a chance to check me out physically and psychologically.

At one point, I was questioned by a so-called psychiatrist who had a reputation of being psychotic himself. Wait 'till you see what happened next. I was talking to this *shrink* about my being in prison and told him how I thought the whole thing was wrong. I was here because of a *marital* problem with my wife, but I was going to do time because of a federal felony conviction.

Then we talked about my children, and of course, that wrenched my heart. You see, I had promised my kids they wouldn't have to go back to *that house*, as they put it, and now I realized I had let them down. I had been tricked into coming back to Pennsylvania, on the pretense of reconciliation, but I wound up getting arrested and now my kids were suffering because of it.

The shrink then asked me about my other daughter, Jaimée, whom I had tragically lost in the dam break just before she turned two years old. While explaining what had happened, my emotions rose up within me. And dredging up grief at such a time as this was just too much to bear. The tears began to flow as I reflected on those difficult days.

That's when the shrink went crazy on me! He acted like a psychotic nut. He started throwing pencils and screaming and waving his arms, shouting, "That's all! That's all!! Get him out of here. Get him out of here. He's not going to pull this @#&* on me. Get him to M.H.U. right NOW!" Later I found out M.H.U. stood for Mental Health Unit, and it was the most dreaded of all places in the prison. It was even worse than solitary confinement. Let me explain . . .

MENTAL HEALTH UNIT

M.H.U. was located directly above the bakery and kitchen on the second floor. The reason I'm sharing about the architectural layout here is that it will help you better understand the story I'll be telling you later.

Anyway, I entered M.H.U. and saw that it was one big room with ten or twelve cells tucked away on each of the three sides of the room. The fourth side housed the supervising guard who sat by a large desk. I was escorted to the left side of the room and pushed into the fourth cell. The door slammed shut behind me. Inside, was a cot suspended by two chains with the back hinged to the wall and everything was so sterile.

As I looked around, my first thought was, "Where's the mattress?" Then I heard a guard behind me yell, "Get all your @#&* clothes off."

I protested, "I've already been strip searched."

He fired back, "I didn't ask you about your @#&* opinion. I said, get your @#&* clothes off!"

My mind raced. I kept thinking about the horror stories I had heard, about men in P.O.W. camps being raped. Even if I tried to fight my way out of this, where could I go? I saw the guard on duty sitting at the desk, but he seemed far removed from my situation.

Well, I should have obeyed orders immediately, but I needed to stall for time; I had to see what was going to happen next. So I stripped to my undershorts while the guard was trying to stuff a cloth bag in between the bars.

"Put them in here," he snapped. I put my clothes in the bag.

"I told you, *all* of them!" I looked at him in disbelief as I slowly removed my shorts and also put them in the bag. I thought for sure something weird was going to happen, and I was ready to fight. But to my surprise, he just took the bag and walked away.

I looked at the bunk and stood there wondering what was next. It was stainless steel with two-inch sides. I figured the sides must have been there to keep the mattress in place when the bed was folded up against the wall on its hinges. It was all very strange, and I still couldn't understand why I had to give up my clothes.

WAITING IN THE RAW

Once again it struck me: I remembered where I was. I was in prison. I thought, "This will probably be just like navy boot camp. They'll bring me some old green or grey prison outfit that won't be the right size and that's what I'll have to wear from now on. Yeah. That's it; piece of cake."

Then I saw the guard returning with some wide straps and chains. "My God in Heaven!" I thought. "What is this craziness?!"

The first thing that came to mind was, "O.K. fool. You can come on in here, but the fight is really gonna be on when you do." I think he must have seen it in my eyes. He must have had a lot of experience with folks like me because he stood there just looking at me. I mean he was really staring.

Then he turned toward the big desk near the doorway, which made the great big guard get up and amble his way over to us. He looked like some big old bull calf as he shuffled up to the first guard. Then they both stood and stared. I was in nothing but my skin, and feeling like some caged animal. I didn't know what to think but I was getting edgy with all the gawking.

A door opened across the room and another guard came in. At this point, I thought that being beaten and knocked out wasn't worth the fight unless of course, it was for self-protection against a sexual violation. If it came down to that they'd have to knock me unconscious.

The first guard drawled, "Are you going to give us any trouble?"

"Well that depends on what you're gonna do," I responded.

He said, "What *you're* gonna do is lie down on the bunk. If you can do that for us you won't get hurt, but if it's trouble you want we can supply it for ya and plenty of it."

I laid back on the hard, steel bunk and they proceeded to put the wide straps over me, connecting the chains to the underside of the bed. When I was secured, they abruptly left and went back to their posts.

So, there I was and so miserable at that. At least the thing I feared most didn't happen. Escaping that calmed me down. But I was still angry. My thoughts turned back to my wife and I started cussing at her in my mind. I imagined all sorts of ways I could get even with her. I thought if I could ever get the chance, I'd rip her heart out and hang it on a string like a dead chicken. In fact, I vowed that I would! (I had temporarily forgotten the promise I made to God.) Finally, sheer exhaustion took over and I fell asleep on that cold piece of stainless steel.

THE THORAZINE MAN

I had about a two-hour nap but it felt more like five minutes. I was awakened by the sounds of people talking, screaming, laughing, and crying. Apparently, it was time for the "Thorazine Man". Thorazine is administered to people (like me) to keep them from going crazy or jumping off the deep end. It's an aggression inhibitor that reduces violent behavior but it apparently turns the recipient into a passive vegetable, and it's quite addictive too.

I thank God for taking such good care of me, even in this situation. When "the Doc" came in to see me, he found me to be very quiet and calm. He said, "You look pretty good today boy. You seem to be getting along quite well, huh?" Speaking of the Thorazine he said, "You don't really need one of these this time 'round, do you?"

My voice came out as smooth and intelligent sounding as I could make it: "No sir."

He walked away.

I lay there while the time ticked on, and then shift change happened. In came a big red-headed guard. His smile looked like it was pasted on his face.

He made himself scarce during the first part of the shift, but he came back again at midnight on rounds. In the middle of the quiet, he slipped me a greeting: "How ya doin' fella?"

"Alright, I guess," I answered. "Say, what do you know about the Doc? And what about those shots he was handing out?"

"Red" was his name and he told me all about the Thorazine Man. He said as long as a person was quiet, he could avoid him and his treatments. That was really helpful information and I was glad to get it.

I found out later that Red was a certified Gideon and also had his own business on the side. He stayed in trouble all the time, though, for being too nice to the prisoners. After I got out of M.H.U. and into the general population, Red and I became pretty good friends. In fact, we still keep in touch to this day. Twice he even drove the ten and a half hour, six hundred mile trip from Pittsburgh to Toccoa to visit me.

As for being in the mental ward, it turns out everyone was unstrapped at some point, long enough to eat meals and wash. Wash? Yes, we would have to wash ourselves and our metal bunks because of the exercise of our bodily functions that occurred while we were fastened down.

CHAPTER TWENTY-SEVEN

GETTING SICK OF M.H.U.

I had been in M.H.U. four or five days when the shrink came to see me again. I guess I was seized by the moment and didn't waste any time speaking up. I wanted out! And I told him so. But that's not what he wanted to hear. He couldn't have spent more than a minute or two with me before he walked away cussing and mumbling. I realized I had made a big mistake. The only way I was going to get off this psyche ward was to remain calm, quiet, and humble, just like Red said. After I had blown it I thought to myself, "Geez Louise. It was all explained to me. I was told how to act but no. I had to go and open my big mouth. Who knows when I'll get out now."

Meanwhile, the noises coming out of those cells were pathetic. The more the inmates carried on, the more the guards liked it. As the mayhem escalated, the guards haunted and taunted all the more. They'd throw apples, tomatoes, or bananas at the bars, causing splatter to fall out on the naked captives. Seventy-five percent of the time it was a real caged animal act.

Another week and a half went by. Then one day I saw the Doc stop one of the guards during his rounds. He had motioned to me while they talked. When he left, the guard came over and told me I was about to be let out of the straps but they'd be watching me very closely. Then he said the most unexpected thing: "I know you aren't supposed to be here, but there isn't anything I can do about it. If you'll stay quiet and real submissive to the Doc when he comes around, he's liable to turn you loose."

140

Believe me, that was the news I'd been waiting for. I wanted to do whatever was necessary, because I believe Hell couldn't have been much worse, especially considering those blood-curdling sounds that rocked on day and night. So I waited quietly and believed my time would soon come. Red mentioned he had heard I was going to "general pop", (General population.)

Well, it happened just like Red had said. My time finally arrived. But before my release, I was interviewed one more time. And this time, it was to help me understand the transition I was about to make into the mass population of the prison. I have to say, I couldn't have been prepared enough for what lay ahead. I was about to become acclimated into prison life. What a realization. All in all, I was sure it would be far better than M.H.U.

THE REALITY OF PRISON

I was in a real prison now, with real prisoners and it was everything I had expected it to be. I saw row after row of cells, back to back. Cells were stacked like layer cakes, one on top of another, four stories high. It was like a large city compared to M.H.U.

God definitely had me in a very captivating place. The time for play acting was over. There was no one to impress here, so going along with the crowd and leaving Jesus behind would have been an easy road to take. Behaving just like everyone else could have helped me because in prison, Jesus freaks are not very popular. But I also knew blending in was not an option for me. It wasn't even a consideration. How much I actually blended in would remain to be seen.

Just then, I thought of Jonah's plight. Jonah had managed to get himself into a whale's belly. What a trap *that* was! When he finally did get out of there, he gained back his freedom. I wondered how long it would be before I'd ever gain my freedom again. Getting out of M.H.U. did give me back a measure of it, but sadly, I was still incarcerated.

TRUE FREEDOM

Generally speaking, freedom is what you make of it. That's what I told some of the "unsaved" inmates, especially those who were getting out soon. They were looking at their release as the ultimate freedom. I would tell them: "You think you'll be free, but you'll still be a prisoner. You won't be controlled by the warden anymore, but you'll be hounded by Satan. He's going to do everything he can to keep you in bondage. And you won't be able to enjoy your freedom as long as you give in to his temptations. You will *think* you're free, but you'll be dancing to his tune; you'll be under his control, just like you're controlled by the warden right now."

I really wanted them to understand their position in God and the total freedom they could have in Him. I had danced to Satan's tunes for many years. I thought that being free meant I could live any way I wanted to, and that being imprisoned represented the loss of that freedom. I didn't know there was a better way. I learned that true freedom in life comes only when we accept forgiveness for our sinfulness, paid for by Jesus Christ, who was crucified on the cross for our sakes.

The book of John, chapter eight, tells us how this all works: Jesus had just met some men bringing a naked woman down the street and they were going to stone her to death. They said she had been caught in adultery, and they wanted her to be punished to the full extent of the law. When Jesus asked them who among them had never sinned, they couldn't answer Him.

Jesus then said, ***"Let any one of you who is without sin be the first to throw a stone at her,"*** (vs. 7; NIV). The passage goes on to say that Jesus stooped down and wrote on the ground, and those who were condemning the woman began to leave, one at a time; the older ones first, then the younger ones, until only Jesus was left with the woman still standing there.

Jesus straightened up and asked her, "Woman, where are they? Has no one condemned you?"

"No one, sir," she said.

"Then neither do I condemn you," Jesus declared. "Go now and leave your life of sin," (Vs 10, 11).

Jesus later said, ***"I tell you truthfully, everyone who sins is a slave to sin, and a slave has no permanent place in the family, but a son belongs to it forever. So if the Son sets you free, you will be free indeed,"*** (vs 34-36).

"If you hold to my teaching, you are really my disciples. Then you will know the truth, and the truth will set you free," (vs 31, 32).

This is the great and true freedom I've been talking about. It comes through Christ alone, but we must walk in His truths and apply them daily to our lives. Only then can we be free indeed.

I had danced with the Devil on the other side of that freedom for a long, long time. My failures had overshadowed me. Now, I longed for a sense of the same freedom Jesus was offering this woman.

HOME SWEET HOME

Speaking of wardens, ours was as mean as Satan himself which made even the six and seven-foot guards afraid of him. I couldn't understand how a little man could instill so much fear in people. Eventually, though, I found out why. I'll share more about that later. But first, let me tell you about my new home.

The guard took me to my cell; I was to be housed in one of those multi-layered cages. As we approached range number 14, we went up a few flights of stairs to my cell block. My cell number was "0", So that's who I became: #0-14.

The rows of ranges were set back to back and were completely separated by a hidden, four-foot wide alley-way. This enclosed corridor contained miles and miles of plumbing that hooked into each of the individual cells.

When we got to my cell the guard said, "Here you are. Hope you enjoy your new home." I stepped inside and stood facing the inner wall. Once again, that dreaded, clang rang in my ears as the door shut tight behind me. I wanted to deny it all, at least for a few moments. Maybe there was a chance that I was dreaming. So I didn't turn around. I didn't want to see that locked door behind me. It was proof that my freedom really had been snatched away.

If I had had a sense of awe over how huge this place was as I walked through the building, that wonderment was now gone. Only fear and loneliness remained, along with the all too familiar feelings of depression. Here I was in a place I never thought I'd be, and it was to become my home; my new *home sweet home.*

CHAPTER TWENTY-EIGHT

LIFE ON THE RANGE

I spent a lot of time alone at first, trying not to think about where I was or what was going on around me. This place was weird and wild, and it definitely brought out the depravity of man. And the folks that ran the place were not much better.

It was dreadful. There was constant fighting, and people were getting hurt. Alcohol in the form of homebrew was being made in secret places and consumed along with marijuana that was being smuggled in by men on work release programs, (they worked outside of the prison). Furthermore, immorality was going on all the time; homosexual acts were almost a daily recreation for many.

And some of the contraband was brought in by a few of the guards! These guards would steal food from the kitchen or offer other kinds of contraband in exchange for sexual favors. Yes, that's exactly what I said: sexual favors. When I thought of all the shameful activities so rampant on the inside, I could see how totally different life was going to be compared to living on the outside. This lifestyle was not only accepted, but it was also exploited.

My real burden, though, was over the scarcity of Bibles and the absence of any Christian or religious conversation. How I longed to hear the Gospel freely spoken, and see the good news of Jesus Christ at work in the lives of these men.

Then God began to work in my life. He drew my attention to what I needed to be doing; I needed to be reaching out to these lost souls in this so-called prison culture. It was a real calling from the Lord. So in the weeks to follow, I started talking to the men about Jesus.

Prison is an awful place to be but listen: if you're reading this and you don't know Jesus as your Savior and Lord, then you are in a prison that's worse than the one these men were in. Honestly, I would rather spend my life in prison as a child of God, than live freely and die, never having accepted Christ as my Savior.

The Bible says, **"For all have sinned and come short of the glory of God,"** (Romans 3:23). That's everybody! Your only way out of this mess is to ask Christ to forgive you and come into your heart as your Lord and Master. If I haven't made this clear, then please find someone who knows Christ and can make it clear for you. Tell them your need. It's very important. It's truly a matter of life and death. Without Christ, you'll never know the joy of complete freedom in Him, and you'll never enter the kingdom of God.

MY OLD BIBLE

I stood there in my new "home on the range" thinking, "woe is me". Then I realized that clutched there in my right hand was my dear old, cloth- covered Bible. What a friend it had been to me already. But what a blessing it was that the guards let me keep it. Was that unimaginable? Yes. It was unbelievable! But there it was at my side. God is so good.

I was later told that keeping that Bible was a tremendous oversight on someone's part because nothing personal is allowed to be kept, not even a Bible. They had actually searched through my Bible, and its old cloth cover, looking in all the hidden places for drugs. When they had found nothing, they flipped it at me and said contemptuously, "You can betcha, if you had *anything* in there, I guarantee we would have found it!"

It was their pride that blinded them to the fact that the most powerful item I could have, was the one they let me keep! So I managed to hang on to it during the entire time I was imprisoned.

That old Bible was my friend in time of need, my solace when I was down, my truth when I needed a leg to stand on, my weapon when I needed to fight off the enemy, and my textbook when I wanted to share the love of Christ with others. God's Word was a true comfort, and not just spiritually speaking. It was also a physical comfort because I used it as my pillow.

In spite of the huge population numbered in the hundreds, there were only about 30 pillows to go around. Many times, pillows were bought, stolen, gambled over, traded, sold, fought for, and even *willed*, in the event of the death of its owner. Wow! How crazy is that? But God supplied me with a pillow of my very own, with the complete Word of God right inside!

SO WHAT ON EARTH WAS MY PURPOSE NOW?

I have to say, this place was a nightmare yet I found humor in it too. At times, the goings-on were even laughable. An outsider wouldn't have believed me in a million years. I would have come off like I was joking or lying. But it was all true. I know, because this stuff happened to me.

I was laughing in a sad sort of way, though, because it was all so surreal. This God-forsaken place was my residence now. Everything else eroded away. Time transformed the unreal into reality and I was now part of the system. When I stopped to realize that, it shook me to my very core. This was not the reality I used to know.

Prison is another complete world hiding away behind walls. It's like a world within a world. It's the other side of freedom . . . and it is very real.

Just for a moment, think of a person on the outside who drives by the exterior wall of the prison each day, going about their business. That person gets just as accustomed to seeing the institution from the outside, as a trapped man does from the inside. They might say, "See, that's the prison," yet never see anything except a pile of stone and mortar. They may never realize that there are living, breathing, human souls in there who feel as dead and forgotten as that cold, grey building.

I found out that each inmate has a warm heart beating inside his breast. Each one has been birthed by a Mom, somewhere, who still loves her jailed child. The heartache behind those walls is titanic in size, and the many painful stories of the men and women there couldn't be entirely told, even in a lifetime.

Why, why, why, do people turn to lives of crime? Many may have an answer but they're really just excuses. The absence of God in a person's life is the only real answer. I determined that if I were to spend the rest of my life in prison, I would spend it helping men get free through knowing Jesus Christ. Even from behind bars, a man can find his way back from the other side of freedom; free in spirit and no longer condemned by Almighty God. I believe God was saying, "I have called you for this purpose, son, and you are finally in a place where I can help you grow into that calling. Do not be afraid, because I Am with you."

IS THE GLASS HALF FULL?

I once heard a couple of old expressions that go like this:

> Two men locked in a prison cell
> One saw Heaven and one saw Hell

and:

> Two men locked outside of prison bars
> One saw mud, the other saw stars

You know, if I can get a man to "look up" and get away from his depression, he'll be able to see clearly enough to want to see Christ. I want men to cast their gaze toward Heaven, not Hell. That a man would look down at his shoelaces all the time is what Satan wants. That's how he gets people to focus on themselves instead of on God. But it doesn't have to be that way. I guess these sayings have stuck with me, even though I've probably taken them out of context, but it's kind of like asking, "Is the glass half full or half empty?" I try to encourage folks to see the glass half full.

There's another well known expression that says, "You can't win a man to the Lord Jesus Christ until you win him to yourself." If I was going to get a man to look up, he would first have to like me and what I stood for, or he wouldn't want what I had to offer.

I was glad to discover a way to reach out and make friends in prison. Here's how it worked: Even though I've never been much for cards, I started playing games like Spades, Hearts, Fish, and Poker. I wasn't much good at it except for the game of Spades and after a while, some of the hard-core guys were asking me to be their partner. When that happened, I knew I had won their friendship and respect. And that's when I met a guy named *Doc.* I need to tell you about him.

CHAPTER TWENTY-NINE

DOC

Doc had been in and out of prison ever since he came back from Viet Nam. He had some hard experiences during the war that he could never quite overcome. It made him mean and rough but at the same time, there was a sweet tenderness about him.

Doc had two little girls as I did, but he knew he'd be in prison for the rest of his life and could never again look after them the way he wanted to. He cared a lot about their lives and their reputations. So he let his ex-wife's new husband adopt them; they even took the man's last name. It took a loving heart to give them up.

Pride can damage a life in many ways, but it can also damage the lives of others. No matter what Doc did to wind up in prison, I'll always respect him for swallowing that pride and giving his little girls a better chance in life. Allowing their last name to change had to be very hard and painful, yet he loved his girls and even his wife enough to let them go, so they could move on. It was the most unselfish and gracious thing a daddy could do.

Doc was a good friend to me; one of the closest friends I ever had in there, even though he was a hard-core kind of guy. He taught me a lot of tricks in prison, like how to hang a picture on a solid steel wall.

Think about it. How would you do it? After I saw it done, I realized it was amazingly simple. You just put a couple of dabs of toothpaste on the back of your photo and presto: It'll stick. When you want to move the picture to a different spot, you simply re-wet the toothpaste to make it pliable again and then rehang it.

Yes, doc was a gem. He sort of looked out for me, too, and helped me along the way.

A SCARY STORY One day, Doc brought me a newspaper. That was a real treat because they were pretty scarce in there. But he showed me an article about two little girls and their Mother. (I still have that article today - see below.) The story really made us panic because we feared it could have been about either of our own families.

Maine Man is Convicted in Oven Death of Child, 4

BANGOR, Maine (UPI) – A judge has rejected an insanity defense and convicted a man of murder for burning his girlfriend's daughter in an electric oven because he thought she was the devil.

A superior Court Judge Bruce Chandler yesterday convicted John Lane, 37, in the death last year of Angela Palmer, 4, who neighbors over heard screaming "Let me out! Let me out!" before her charred body was found in an oven jammed shut with a chair.

Lane faces a possible life prison term when he is sentenced Friday.

Lane's defense lawyer E. James Burke argued yesterday that the death occurred during an exorcism.

While chandler concede Lane might have been suffering from mental problems, he said there was enough evidence to hold him accountable.

The death occurred in an Auburn apartment where Land and Palmer lived with Angela and her 6-year old sister, Sarah.

Here's a follow up on that story:

Security Tight at Trial in Girl's Oven Death

BANGOR, Maine (UPI) – Tight security was ordered for today's trial of a couple accused of burning a 4-year old girl to death in an electric oven.

A dozen deputies were assigned to patrol Penobscot County Superior Court with metal detectors in operation at several checkpoints, said Sheriff Carl Andrews.

"We are concerned about any individual who might want to short-cut the criminal justice system" in the murder trial of John Lane, 36, and his girlfriend, Cynthia Palmer, 29, of Lewiston. They are accused of killing Ms. Palmer's daughter from a previous marriage, Angela, Andrews said.

The trial is being held in Bangor, 100 miles from the scene of the incident, because lawyers for the defendants won a change of venue.

"It is reasonably clear that due to the nature of the crime . . . it would be very difficult, if not impossible, to maintain proper security and decorum of the trial in the Androscoggin County Courthouse," defense attorney James E. Burke said.

Neighbors had reported loud religious music coming from the Lewiston apartment where Lane and Palmer lived with Palmer's two daughters, Angela and Sarah.

On Oct. 27, 1984, neighbors smelled acrid smoke seeping out of the apartment, and heard a child's voice shouting, "Let me out, Daddy, let me out."

When police arrived, they found the kitchen oven turned on with the door jammed shut with a kitchen chair. When they opened the door, they found the charred body of the girl.

During a bail hearing last February, a transcript of a confession allegedly obtained from Lane was read in court. Lane allegedly told police he believed the girl was the devil, and that she was going to kill members of the family.

"I threw her in the oven . . . she was going to kill us," Lane reportedly said.

Even though Doc and I were two men who tried to see the glass as half full, we still had our dreadful moments. It wasn't easy by any means, to keep looking upward toward Heaven instead of toward the things of Hell.

MY TWO LITTLE GIRLS

I have always been grateful to God that I was able to keep pictures of my two little girls with me. I would sit and stare at them for hours. Although I was always happy to look at them, sometimes it added to the depression I felt being away from them. But I had to go on no matter what lay ahead. There really weren't any other choices other than suicide, and I occasionally thought about that too. One night I stayed up and wrote this poem:

My Little Girls

❀

Two little pictures
hanging on the wall.
I guess that I will never again
see them at all.
I feel a million miles from them
in this prison cell.
And yet I'm only two doors down
from a living Hell

❀

❀

Oh, how my heart burns now,
unquenchably, in pain.
Can it be true
that I'll never hold them again?
The one who loved to hold
the "little" finger of my hand;
she's held it every since the day
she first learned to stand.

❀

continued . . .

❦

The other one would snuggle up
and nibble at my ear.
And now for wondering
how they are
I live in constant fear.
If ever a man has loved his child,
these little ones own my heart.
And never in my wildest dreams,
did I think we'd be apart.

❦

With toothpaste dabs, I glued the
pictures there upon the wall.
And it's the only spot in here
with any warmth at all.
And though the air here freezes
the water where it stands,
there's nothing colder
than to think
I'll never hold their hands.

❦

Two little pictures
hanging on the wall.
Is this all there is to living,
after all!

I would try death, to do away
with all the pain.
But I will hold to hopeless hope
that I may see them again.

❦

Though the days go by
and turn to years,
I must believe some way
that God in mercy, and in love,
will bring about the day.
Although my hair be silver,
hanging o'er a wrinkled brow.
I'll hold them once more
in my arms,
the way I want to now.

❦

As long as rivers flow downhill,
and there's a sun above,
I must hold on to hopeless hope,
because of God's great love.
He will sustain me in my sorrow,
and comfort all my pain,
until the pictures are *alive*
and in my arms again!

rdVeer© October 1985

154

CHAPTER THIRTY

THE ECONOMY AND ETHICS OF "GIVING"

It was my friend Doc Cornelius that got me a job in the bakery. Of course, I didn't receive a paycheck for it. There's no cash system in prison, but there is a barter system. My so-called pay for five to eight hours of labor every day was two bags of tobacco and two packs of rolling papers per week. Those were tradable for one pack of regular, commercial (tailor-made) cigarettes. These, in turn, were thought of as money for such things as hair cuts, laundry, books, etc. which could be bought with them.

If a prisoner had a family that took care of him, then, of course, there wasn't a problem with getting material things. The family simply dropped off items by way of the front desk. For other inmates who had been in prison a long while, whose families may have given up trying to visit or even remember them, the barter system was all that was left.

It wouldn't make sense to someone on the outside but it was very serious business for those of us on the inside. As for me, I didn't smoke, so I had a pack of cigarettes to deal with each week. It didn't go very far so I had to be wise with my choices.

Once, I bought a t-shirt from an inmate who was going home soon. I guess that was extravagant, but I still have that shirt today. It serves as a worn out reminder of what life was like back then.

Now, when I look at all I possess, I feel like a very wealthy man, but don't get me wrong. Material possessions are not my mainstay. I'm not interested in having a fortune. Even if I did, I know I can't take it with me. I'd just be cluttering up Heaven with unnecessary earthly junk.

So I've come to appreciate what I have and would gladly give away the little bit I do have, to help someone in need. And yes, I have been down and pretty low at times, but I've always been able to help others. Even when others have had more than me, I've still tried to help them when I could. Isn't that what really makes life worthwhile? I think so.

Many of my well-meaning family and friends have criticized me for this philanthropical attitude, but God has supplied me with so much--over and above my needs--that I can't make material possessions important enough to hang on to, whether I'm well off in the moment or not.

At the same time, I understand the need to be responsible for my family, so I do not give away their reserves to help someone else. My family does come first. I do my part when I can. I'm not lazy. I do get out there and work with the best of them, but all in all, I trust God to take care of me and mine, saving room to help others too.

You ask, "How does it all work?" My answer is simple: "Do you want to *have?* Then *give!*" This is a biblical principle that works. Luke 6:38 says, ***"Give, and it shall be given unto you; good measure, pressed down, and shaken together, and running over, shall men give into your bosom. For with the same measure that ye measure, it shall be measured back to you,"*** (KJV).

MY DAY JOB

Working in the bakery was a real privilege for me. I had been a cook and a baker in the Navy, so this jailhouse job was great. I had to get up very early each morning, about 4:30 AM as I remember, but that was fine because I've always been an early riser. I enjoyed having something to do at that time of day. Even more so, I enjoyed the freedom of being out of my cell for a few hours.

The bakery was attached to the kitchen so it was a big room. It was divided into two sections: the bakery took up one half and the kitchen took up the other half. Each side was about 40 by 40 feet. (Just guessing.) After being cooped up in a six by nine-foot cell all day, it was great to have all that freedom and all that space to walk around in.

I have to say, too, that I've always been kind of a *clean freak*. I used to use my free time at home to clean; I'd get bursts of energy and scrub down the entire kitchen from end to end.

Well, one Saturday afternoon, I got into one of those cleaning moods while at the bakery. Although clean up procedures were routine, our duties were much lighter on the weekends so I was looking to make work. Therefore I decided to stay longer; I didn't want to go back to my cell.

Besides that, I was feeling bored, and sure enough didn't want to face another long, lonely weekend with nothing to do. So I got real ambitious that day and started in on some deep cleaning; some downright scrubbing. I wanted to make the whole place gleam like a hospital operating room.

I got out some brushes, some steel wool, some cleanser, and whatever else I could find. My enthusiasm must have been infectious because it affected the whole bakery crew. Pretty soon all thirteen of us were scurrying around like squirrels, dedicated to our new found task of overhauling our work area.

In a corner of the room, there was a rack, about five feet long and six or seven feet high with five or six shelves. I removed several 25-pound bags of flour and sugar and dragged the unit away from the wall. The walls were made of ceramic tile like those found in commercial restrooms. As I remember, the tiles had sort of a creamy color, and the more I scrubbed, the better they looked. After a good, long while, my hard work had paid off. The tiles looked considerably lighter; not creamy at all but stark white!

THE BAKERY RAID

I continued going over one tile after the next, covering more and more area. Then I noticed a door in the wall. The door was made of a rusty, quarter- inch, stainless steel and had a padlock hanging from it that wasn't fastened. "Mmm," I thought. "I'd like to know where that goes." But wisdom said, "Hey dummy. You're in a prison. Don't mess with it." I decided not to open it. I figured it couldn't have been too important if it wasn't even locked, so I just kept scrubbing.

I can't tell you how astonished I was by what happened next. In an instant, the whole crew was overwhelmed by guards who came bursting into the bakery. It was frightening to be cleaning away, and then suddenly have the whole scene change. One minute we were enjoying a kind of pseudo-freedom and the next minute, it was all over. Our serenity was violently snatched away.

They grabbed us and slammed us against the wall, prodding and pulling at us in a shake-down. It all happened so fast; it was beyond belief. We were handcuffed and pushed aside so more guards could come in. Then we were all taken away.

Even more surprising was that as we were going out, the press was coming in! The whole chain of events barely registered in my mind. But what I did know is that in the blink of an eye, all thirteen of us found ourselves in solitary confinement.

SOLITARY CONFINEMENT

The "solitary cells" were in a section all on their own. They were four stories high and faced a blank wall. You could never see anything except for a guard that might walk by on the cat-walk once in a while. It was definitely a place of isolation.

Each of us was delivered to our individual little cells. Then the guards took us one at a time, back to our home cells to get our belongings. I breathed a sigh of thanks to the Lord because somehow, I was allowed to keep my Bible and my daughters' pictures. These were the only items in the whole wide world that held any importance for me. During my time in prison, no matter where I was housed, I would either sit and read or stare at my girls for hours, wondering if I would ever see them again. Yet I trusted God's larger plan: I believed I would see them again one day.

I talked with many men who had been locked up for a long time. They said they couldn't even remember the faces of their loved ones anymore. I surely didn't want that to happen to me. Thank God that by His grace, it didn't.

I don't know when my turn came to go packing, but there was a lot of yelling going on amongst us while we waited. That's because the thirteen of us were not kept next to each other. We were scattered throughout the cell block. Later, I discovered this was strategically arranged to prevent us from matching stories and plotting lies about what happened in the bakery. In fact, that's what came out in the media. But it was all a big cover-up. The prison authorities didn't want us to know what they were doing to us.

During the days and weeks that followed, we were periodically taken into the assistant warden's office and questioned. We had to wear orange coveralls and leg chains. We also had to wear a wide webbed belt that buckled and locked behind our back. Attached to it were rings, one on each side near our waist. The rings were chained to our arms, *plus*, we had to wear handcuffs. Wow. I was wondering who we were supposed to have killed?!

CHAPTER THIRTY-ONE

MEETING WITH THE WARDEN

The first time I was questioned, I decided to make use of lessons gleaned from M.H.U. There, I had learned how to be polite, quiet, and gentlemanly.

They put me in a regular straight-backed office chair and proceeded to study me as if I were a rare species of some kind. Finally, the warden said to the assistant warden, "Yeah . . . huh . . . look at that *pretty boy smile.* I'll wipe that !#$!&* thing off his face before he leaves here!"

Oh boy. I knew I was in for it. I had heard about this warden's reputation, and now I was going to get a sample of it.

They started their questioning, but none of it made any sense. They wanted me to tell them how long I had been digging my way out of the bakery in order to escape. I was baffled. I had absolutely no idea what they were talking about.

Here's what I learned much later: The day I was cleaning the kitchen, I had found a steel door. I didn't know that behind it was an earthen floor and brick walls that were three stories high. They connected to the floor underneath the Mental Health Unit.

I believe it was said that the walls were five layers thick, but three layers had already been dug out, and there were pancake turners and can openers laying there which had been used to scrape out the mortar. So, a legitimate prison escape had been attempted, but *I* certainly didn't know anything about it. I guess whoever planned it had left me out.

Let me tell you what else they found. Behind the door was a small golden colored, three-gallon lard can

161

full of cooking oil. The oil had a floating plastic lid from a two-pound coffee can, and in the lid was a hole with a strand of braid from a floor mop; it was a makeshift wick. So this lard can was actually used as a large candle and the whole system behind that steel door was set up to make moonshine. That's the real reason it was all there, but the Warden wanted details about our planning a prison escape.

During the questioning, I was grabbed by the back of my knees and pulled forward until I was barely sitting on the front edge of my chair. In this position, a lead-weighted baton was swung between my legs, hitting the fringes of my orange clothing, and coming dangerously close to my tender, vital body parts. They swung a billy club at me too, touching the hair hanging over my forehead, and sometimes it brushed my nose. It was very intimidating.

Later, I heard that all of us had gone through the same sort of treatment. They said someone outside our *gang* had supposedly squealed on us for trying to make a getaway, and since I was one of the guilty thirteen, I might as well confess. We were all forced to sign a form that said if only *one* person out of the group confessed to this "crime", the entire crew would get an extra seven-and-a-half years added to his sentence. It would be an automatic conviction, without a trial. Period!

A JAILHOUSE MINISTRY IS BORN

It was during my solitary confinement experience following that so-called "prison break" attempt that I began to blossom as a preacher. About a week after being dumped there, I was singing the old songs I used to sing back in church. I had been reading my Bible this particular day, and the music just poured out of me. That's when I got the nickname "Preacher Man". From a lower level, somebody hollered, "Hey Preacher Man, it's Sunday. How 'bout a little preachin'?"

I didn't respond because I wasn't sure if the guy was heckling me or if he was serious, so I softly hummed the tune of another song, *Open My Eyes That I May See*. If he had been picking on my singing, then toning it down would have helped the situation and maybe he would have shut up, but in prison I learned, you shouldn't fail to respond.

He called out again, "What about it Preach? Thanksgiving and Christmas is comin' and we be in here for a long, long time. Ya need to bring us some preachin'!"

"Are you serious?" I called back.

"Yeah!"

I agreed but I wanted to sing a bit more, so I asked if any of them knew any Gospel songs, and when they named a few we began to sing them. Then I got to preaching a little about what I had just been reading, and that's how my ministry began. In time, they had even elevated me to *Pastor*, but I admit, it was humbling and I was self-conscious about it.

After that, they asked me to preach for them more often and we had some really good times, talking about the Bible. I was very thankful to have mine with me. I was glad to have a chance to do God's work. I became very aware of the importance of His Word, and I realized that with it, I had plenty to offer the inmates.

Oh, I know all about jailhouse conversions. Everyone knows they're mostly phony and no one respects them. They're only employed to gain some administrative advantage. But I also know first-hand that when a real bad guy responds honestly to an invitation to accept Christ, you can be sure he means serious business, and it will make an impression on others. Those are the kind of conversions that thrill my heart down to my soul.

THE BAKER'S DOZEN

After many weeks of solitary, the surprising day came. The guards came in and told us to pack up 'cause we were going back to general pop. We were also told someone in the Baker's Dozen gang had confessed.

"No!" I thought. "It can't be. If that were true, the squealer would have told us what was up, wouldn't he"?

A few days later, the truth came out; at least some of it. The one who talked had confessed to what he had really done, and it wasn't an attempt to escape. He confessed to making homebrew: moonshine. But, what in the world did that have to do with digging tunnels and trying to escape? I couldn't figure it out. Even though we were being released from solitary, the whole thing remained a mystery to me.

The story hit the newspapers as well as the six o'clock news; it ran for days and days on end. Reports echoed out from the media about how we had been questioned, what kinds of things had been discovered, and how we had lied. The headlines read, "Baker's Dozen Captured Before Escape Attempt Completed."

As a kid growing up, I used to like the whole baker's dozen concept. Often, when we bought a dozen donuts, the baker would throw in an extra one. Cool, right? Well, being in *this* baker's dozen was not so cool. The whole thing left me full of questions. There was a big fat curious gap in my understanding and I really wanted to know the truth.

MISSING OUT ON SUPPER

It was only four or five days after being back in my regular cell (in general pop) that I had a new little problem. I was waiting for chow call one evening, but when the time came to go eat, all the cell doors opened (electronically) except mine. I was upset, to say the least. For one thing, I didn't want to go on until morning without a meal, and I had been in solitary for so long, that I was looking forward to getting out of my cramped up space.

I'm ashamed to tell you what happened next, but I lost my cool. Yes, I lost my temper. When the guards found I was locked in, they gave me a very unconcerned response: "Don't sweat it," they said. "We'll be back pretty soon." So I just *went off.* It was a running fit, really. I freaked out and started karate kicking the lock on my cell door.

A lot of time passed and the other men were already coming back from supper but there was still no help in sight. I threw such a hissy-fit that it summoned another guard to my quarters, and guess who it was? My old friend, Red. He had always been good to me and this was no exception. He tried to get the cell door open, but to no avail, so he put an order in for maintenance to take care of it.

Finally, a man came by, looked at the door, went away, and came back with an acetylene torch. He worked on the door for what seemed like hours. The whooshing hiss of the torch flame snapped and cackled its way through years of old paint as the filthy metal dripped red hot liquid droplets onto the cold concrete. They scattered and danced their way across the floor like they were alive. The fire ate its way through the 100-year-old, eighth-inch plate iron. Then, bang! The service man's hammer struck a deadly blow, and the front of the lock clattered onto the floor, sending an acrid stink up into the air for our nostrils to inhale. But I didn't care. I just wanted out!

CHAPTER THIRTY-ONE

THE CAT GOT OUT OF THE BAG

While the maintenance man was working on my cell door, he started talking to me about the recent escape attempt. I guess he was feeling sorry for me being in prison and all, so he was trying to console me. He said, "Awe, man. You shouldn't feel bad about being stuck in here. What about those poor guys that got stuck in solitary? Now, you woulda felt bad if you'd been one of them: you know, the Baker's Dozen?"

I stopped just short of telling him that I was one of them. But I thought I might just dummy-up for a bit and see what he knew about it.

He continued: "Two or three years ago, I had to go up under M.H.U. to take some plumbing apart. One of the crazies up there kind of *went off;* he was nuts. He got a hold of a switch cover and flushed it down the toilet. It got hung up in the "Y joint" and man, I'm tellin' ya; all the plumbing got backed up everywhere! Do you know that space under the psyche ward near the bakery? It was the only way I could get to the problem at the time." I was listening intently.

"Yeah, and that poor sap that got arrested with the other bakers: he ain't never done nothing 'cept make a little homebrew now and then. He ain't no escapee. He just took advantage of the private little hole in the wall that he found. The prison knew it was there all these years. It wasn't nothin' new."

He went on: "What happened was, a week before that so-called escape, two *lifers* had been allowed to go free, by mistake. Yeah! And who's fault was that? The Warden's. These lifers had the same last names as two other guys that were gittin' released. And that ain't all.

167

One guy was black, 'n the other was white. How could he have been so dumb?

"Before this glitch could turn into a really big deal, the Warden dreamed up this Baker's Dozen scheme. This fake escape attempt was fed to the press like bait. But it was all made up; it was jest one big, fat lie! And when it came out that the Baker's Dozen were caught, everybody congratulated the Warden on what a great job he was doing. So while everyone was shaking his hand, his nasty little secret never did come to light. It just sort of fizzled out and disappeared. Can ya imagine that?"

He put down his ratchet and paused, and I sat there taking it all in. I was amazed but I said nothing. We were both captivated by our own thoughts in the moment. Then he added, "Yeah, that's right. And the guys who got turned loose? They were eventually caught. Who can figure it? What a hoot!"

GUILTY UNTIL PROVEN INNOCENT

I thought, "Man alive. The Baker's Dozen thing was just a smoke screen for the Warden's big screw up!" Then I realized what it had cost *me.* I started to steam under the collar, and blurted out, "Yeah, like you said: what a hoot man. But I was one of them. *I* was one of the so-called Baker's Dozen!"

He whipped his head around and stared at me hard. Then he got really nervous. "Mister, hey, please don't tell anyone I talked to you, OK? You gotta promise me you'll keep this to yourself."

Well, I honored my promise as far as telling any guys in general pop, but I did tell a few of my closest buddies. After all, it was a really big deal. It was all over T.V. and the newspapers, and I know our families probably saw it too. As for the administration, I'm sure as long as the prison looked good they didn't care about us. The thirteen arrests made them look like they were really cracking down on escape attempts. We were just a bunch of pawns in their little prison game, and in *this* game, they had to win.

Unless a person's actually been there, they have no idea what it's like being on the other side of freedom. It's one thing to lose basic social freedom, but it's quite another thing to lose your rights as a human being, especially constitutional rights. We are all taught that, by law, a person is innocent until proven guilty. But it's a whole different world once you're accused of a crime, and a judge signs a paper against you. At that point, you are considered guilty until you prove you are innocent. Suddenly, it's a different universe. Many people are locked up who really don't need to be.

MY FRIEND "J.C."

One day, I met a guy in prison named J.C. He was housed next to me in P-14, and I took a real liking to him right from the start. It was just like God to send a believer in Christ my way. J.C. was a gem. He used to loan me his small walkman radio in the evenings so I could listen to Chuck Swindoll.

Swindoll's nightly program was broadcast over radio station WPIT. My whole reality hinged on that 9:00 o'clock hour and the program became my sanity-lifeline. Just before the singers and the wailers would start up on the ranges, I would have good old Chuck to buoy me up with God's Word. His messages made everything more tolerable, and I was probably one of his most faithful listeners, even though he didn't know it. I'd like to say, "Thanks, Chuck. Thanks a million!"

Today, whenever I hear the theme song from that program, great feelings of nostalgia rise up in my heart.

Now let me tell you more about J.C. He was raised in a mental institution because he was the product of two patients who lived there. At the age of ten, J.C. saw his two-year-old brother killed by a guard and another inmate. They kicked him and stomped on him until he was crushed to death.

Additionally, J.C. had never learned to read or write, so he and I spent time together in the Bible. I started with the book of Genesis and the book of John. He loved the stories I shared with him like how the universe began. We went on to explore creation and I drew him some pictures to illustrate the six days God spent, speaking the world into existence. Soon he was drawing pictures which helped him remember Bible passages. From those exercises J.C. learned how to read; his interest in reading grew by leaps and bounds.

After a while, J.C. explained the reason he was locked up. He said it was for traffic tickets! That's what he always believed until the day I began to look over his charges. I learned that he and his room-mate had worked in a 24-hour restaurant on opposite shifts. J.C. usually came home between 7:30 and 8:00 o'clock in the morning.

One particular morning he came home to find his friend packing to move out. It was all very sudden and rather surprising. But the room-mate could not give J.C. a good reason for his move.

It came out later that the room-mate had taken a young boy to the apartment late the night before, and abused him. When it was reported to the police, all the young boy could do was direct them to the place he thought it had happened. He had no name to offer, and not much of a description either.

Later that morning, the police--armed with information--came to J.C.'s place and found him sleeping. They arrested him, handcuffed him, and took him away. He said the trial was short and he was found guilty. Being slightly mentally retarded, and not clearly understanding what was going on, he assumed he was in trouble for the 11 traffic tickets he had. So he accepted the sentence without argument and was now doing 20 years without really knowing what had happened.

When I read his charges, I managed to contact his church, which in turn hired a Christian attorney, who had J.C. released.

Through that effort, God worked a miracle in my life, too. The same Christian attorney looked into my situation and determined that I should have been indited under "domestic law" and not "civil law". My case was a family matter and I should have been tried accordingly.

My case went back to court and the judge agreed with my attorney's conclusions. They dropped my sentence to "time served" and I was released. Hallelujah! God is so amazing!!

I was glad I had met J.C. and enjoyed the time we spent together. The Bible says, **"But be doers of the word, and not hearers only, deceiving yourselves,"** (James 1:22; KJV). This verse will always remind me of J.C. I'm a richer man for knowing him. Yes, I taught J.C, how to read, but he inspired me how to do right. And everything worked out for the best.

Let me tell you a little more about prison life . . .

CHAPTER THIRTY-TWO

CHURCH IN PRISON

The highlight of my week was Thursday when the church team came in to do Bible studies. They would also come in once a month to sing and preach. Some men would go crazy over football games, but for me, football lacked in comparison to those prison church services. It's hard to describe how much they meant to me. Even for the most hardened of hearts, experiencing God's presence was especially fulfilling.

I have to stop right here and give thanks to a very special Pastor, Reverend Gary LaPietra, from Faith Bible Baptist Church in Wilkins Township, Pennsylvania. Gary headed up those services and he and his church were very faithful and dependable. I'd like to say, "May God bless you all and many, many thanks for your love."

One of the members, Dave Herr, became especially dear to me. I caught his sense of caring and real dedication. I haven't talked to Dave for years but I hope to look him up one day. In the meantime, "Thanks, Dave, for showing us men the heart of a real Christian. You're a very special guy and I know God loves you for all you've given us. Your sacrifice was costly for you and your family and we appreciate it so much, as does the Lord. So, God bless you, Dave."

You know, some wounds stink more than others because they have festered longer. Reaching people for Christ takes letting go of one's pride and being willing to go beyond one's self to fill the needs. Our job is to be God's receptionists, and bring patients in no matter what shape they're in. Then God can be the great physician working through us as we serve. That's the essence of what church is supposed to be.

Yes, church in the prison was a great influence on me. While outsiders would say certain individuals were too hard to witness to, the truth is you haven't seen real hardness until you've seen it in prison. By the same token, you haven't seen real brokenness until you've seen it flood over one of those tough, hardened hearts. I have seen many inmates touched by Jesus Christ; the same Jesus that offers salvation to all. Will you receive Him today? And if you've done that already, then would you be willing to share Him today with someone in need?

CHANGED LIVES THROUGH CHRIST

Even though I was incarcerated, God was good to me. He gave me a lot of insight and added to my practical experiences daily. He gave me a vision for helping needy souls, and when I was released I started a prison ministry of my own.

For the longest time, our official ministry slogan was *Ministering to Imprisoned Souls,* but we decided to rename it *Changed Lives Through Christ*. It's the same blueprint really, but it puts the emphasis on the power of God, and not so much on the troubles of man.

The Lord Jesus gave me a soft, caring heart, to notice people who are suffering and in bondage. Some are confined by the system, some by the degrading prison of sin, and some by the complete hopelessness they find in a life without a purpose. Through my own hardships and those of others, I've learned to ask God for His wisdom and perseverance to minister to these lost ones that I meet behind prison doors.

I need to share a few names with you. These are folks that I'll never forget, like Glenn S., Kevin T.,

Steve, Ken who was given 31 to 60 years, Don C., Harry who was saved the day before he went home, Benny B., young Don H. who was a drug dealer since the age of 14, George who was saved two days after Christmas, Napolean A., Lamonte, Jeff R., the Shady-Side Strangler, Nelson G., and Smokie Robinson.

Then there was Brutus. He was the worst of them all. He vowed he would make me his personal *girl*, but God got a hold of him and each one of these others, and they all became my children--so to speak--in Christ Jesus. Each one accepted Christ's love and forgiveness.

STORIES OF BENNY B. AND DON C.

I mentioned Benny B. In my list, above. Benny had been a Jehovah's Witness at one time, but God gloriously brought him out of that. He was saved late one evening and came to me the next morning in a fearfully excited state. He wanted to know what in the world had happened to him.

After his salvation experience, he found himself sitting on the edge of his bunk in the middle of the night saying words that weren't English! Yet, while repeating a phrase over and over again in this strange language, he understood the words to mean, "Thank you for the blood of Jesus; thank you for the blood of Jesus." He was laughing and crying at the same time.

I helped Benny understand God had allowed him to experience the in-filling of the Holy Spirit, which is a marvelous gift. I explained that he had not only been saved but that he had been miraculously baptized in the Holy Ghost and had received the gift of tongues, which was a very special empowerment from God.

After that, Benny decided he wanted to go and live on death row. It was unheard of! But he felt that the men over there were very needy to hear about Jesus. He just wanted to live with them so he could talk to them. The Warden said, "No way! What are you, a crazy man? Have you flipped your lid?! Don't be stupid."

But, Benny was determined. He wouldn't let up. Eventually, the Warden had enough of all the nonsense, and let him go. So, Benny moved over there, and in the first four days, he won two men to the Lord. He continued to be fruitful and effective, and I always prayed God would keep on using him in some evangelical capacity. Praise God!

Another person I mentioned above was Don C. He was also wonderfully saved. He cried when telling about what had happened to him. While he regretted how wicked he had been, he had tears of joy and was amazed at how good God was to pardon him.

He appreciated Jesus so much that he tried to tell everyone about his Lord. But every time he got started, he'd cry. Eventually, word of it reached the Warden who sent guards to fetch him. The Warden wanted to know what the deal was. What was causing all this emotion? Don tried to tell him but--you guessed it. When he started talking, the tears flowed. That was all the Warden needed in order to send Don off to the Mental Health Unit.

I felt sorry for Don because I knew what he would go through there. I had been there myself. I was glad to learn that he weathered it well. After he was released from M.H.U. he still had a tearful tenderness for the Lord. That's because God imparts to us something that is real, and no man can take it away. Coca Cola may claim it, but Don had it; he had *the real thing!*

Fortunately, Don had an early release and went back to his old neighborhood, but not as the *wheeler-*

dealer he once was. Don was a new man with a new story to tell. He told all of his old friends about Jesus. He encouraged them, explaining how their lives could change for the better if they would accept Christ's forgiveness. They could be cleansed of their past and look forward to a better future.

Don was a living example of a changed life through Christ. He was now free from the power of drugs and of street life. If they would listen to the truth they could be free, too. Don had truly escaped *the other side of freedom,* and he wanted nothing more than to show others the way out too.

CHAPTER THIRTY-THREE

GETTING OUT--RENEWING FRIENDSHIPS

The time came for my release from prison, and I knew I was going to need help getting established again. I had barely enough money to buy gas for the 800-mile trip home. I was in a very needy situation and couldn't see how that was going to change.

Before I was incarcerated I had a small home-building business, and I had seven people working for me. One of those men was Ralph Singleton. I decided to look him up; I thought he could help me find work and a place to stay. So I called him up and as we talked on the phone, we cried and chatted about the good old days. Ralph said, "I've never worked for anyone who's been as honest with me as you, and nobody's helped me make as much money as you, either. Yes, I'll help you. You can come to stay with me." So Ralph was there for me, beginning with my first night home.

The very next day, Bob Zeigler called me, and said, "Doug, I'm working at Habersham Plantation Furniture Company as a diesel mechanic. We have an opening here and you need to come by and apply for this truck driving job."

Before I left Toccoa and was arrested, Bob Ziegler had been the manager of Napa Auto Parts, but he wanted to work for me in construction, building houses. So I hired him and we became good friends. Friends are one of the most valuable assets we can have, and Bob was certainly a good friend of mine.

I told Bob I had quit driving truck years ago, but he insisted. I was very uncertain of myself and even more unsure about what my parole officer would say.

As far as I knew, I wasn't even allowed out of the state, but that morning, I applied anyway. Several hours later, I went to the Department of Motor Vehicles and got my Class four driver's permit. I also got permission from my parole officer, which totally blew my mind. The next morning, Habersham Plantation gave me the keys to a fully loaded Mercedes truck, my delivery schedule, and $700 for expenses. Within an hour I was on the road headed for California.

Coming back home from my first run I had enough money to rent a place to live and start life over. After that, everything fell into place. I know it must have been the Lord standing in my place and supplying me with that job because not only were my physical needs met, but the hours on the road all alone gave my emotions time to heal too. You see, when a man gets out of prison, he can't stand to be confined and he can't sit still for very long. Being on the road gave me that calming effect I needed, and I was able to make a good living as well. Yes, God is good!

PEOPLE WHO NEED PEOPLE

Touching lives. That's what it's all about, isn't it? I've always been so amazed at how God has used other people in my life to accomplish good things for me. Ralph gave me a place to sleep, Bob helped me get a job, and in turn, I'm glad to say I had been an encouragement and help to them in times past. I helped Ralph with some of his personal struggles, and I listened to Bob's needs. I became a sounding board regarding his job situation. Later, he moved to Manassas, Virginia--less than an hour from Washington D.C.--to start his own construction business.

Over time, I found that others came to me for advice. Could it be that God was arranging some sort of a counseling ministry for me?

Well, I continued driving truck for a while, but it didn't last. Soon I was back swinging a hammer for a living. And no matter where I went to work, people found me and wanted to draw upon me for help, which I was glad to give.

There was a young man named David who had worked for me previously, but I had to let him go because of his lack of ability in carpentry. One day he came to me, and said, "Doug, I need some fatherly advice about a job I'm considering. I want to go to school in Florida to become an Emergency Medical Technician. And besides that, there's this girl that I'm really attracted to. We've been seeing each other and now I'm wondering if I should ask her to marry me."

I tried to help him sort through his issues, and I can happily say that David did take the job in question, and he did go to school in Florida to become an E.M.T. and a fireman, and, he married the girl of his dreams. I haven't seen many success stories like David's but I'm so glad for his good marriage, good career, and blessed life. I've enjoyed being part of his life and am so glad to be his friend.

Then there was Kathy K. who was referred to me through the Welfare Department. She had some building and construction skills so I put her to work, at least for a while. She had lived a pretty rough life. She had two children out of wedlock and she tried to nurse her problems away with alcohol. As a result, she wound up with several D.U.I.s and lost her drivers license.

As I write this, Kathy is in one of the jails I visit regularly. If she gains permission for a work release program, I may let her work for me again. Maybe this time she'll get her life straightened out and want to really obey the Lord and live right. As long as she keeps trying to be real, I'll keep helping her, and being her friend.

There are others: a guy named Greg was in between jobs and was a good carpenter, so I hired him for a while. We got along well, and he gladly received the encouragement I gave him, praise the Lord. Then there was Bob: (another Bob). He needed a lot of encouragement too. I tried to be a support to him and was thrilled when he went on to build his own business in an old grist mill, selling antiques and various other memorabilia to tourists. God is so good. And when we let Him, He will work in our lives in truly amazing ways.

After being out of prison a couple of years, I got custody of my daughter, Amanda. She made my life truly full again even though my other daughter, Hope, stayed with her mother. Amanda had many girlfriends and they began to call me "Daddy" because most of them had no father in the home. What a great privilege that was for me. I was so glad I could minister to them, too.

IMPRISONED IN A HOUSEHOLD THAT WAS LOST

Have you ever thought about what it's like to be trapped? You can be trapped in a grocery line when you're pressed for time. You can be trapped in a job that you don't like. You can have a flat tire and have no one to call on for help, feeling like no one cares anyway. Or you can be trapped in a family relationship where obligation keeps you involved for the sake of that family.

Being trapped in an annoying situation is one thing, but being forced to live in a distressed home is something else, entirely. Amanda had a young friend from school, Alicia. She asked us over and over if she could come live with us, but of course, I couldn't say yes, although she would have been welcome. She wanted to get away from her abusive Father, but she was trapped in a household where Christ had been shut out, and love had been replaced by selfishness, anger, and abuse. How sad.

Amanda received a letter from her, and it was such a lamentable story. I've included it below--as close to the original as I could--so you might get a feel for the mood of the girl who wrote it. At 15 years old, this girl was scared to death of her father and talked about running away. At the same time, she looked to me for comfort, approval, and guidance.

The *"Daddy"* in capital letters and quotes she is referring to *is me!* The other references are to her own father. The *church* in this letter is the Kingdom Hall, (the church of the Jehovah's Witnesses). Her father forced her to go there on Tuesdays, Saturdays, and Sundays while he sat at home and drank. She tried to come to our church, (the Assemblies of God), but her father said if she did, she would go to Hell for sure. She wanted very badly to be with me and my daughter Amanda, as a family, but I would have needed her mother's permission for that, and the mother was very afraid of the father just like this young girl was. They were all trapped in a terrible situation.

One Saturday evening, the father locked his children in the attic for the whole night, and he locked the mom out of the house so she had to sleep in the car. I don't know how a man can treat his own family that way, especially since it was late in the year and pretty chilly outside. This man had been in and out of prison, brought on by his own making due to his rage and drunkenness. The pain and suffering he brought upon his own household were very real and unnecessary. Undoubtedly, the entrance of Christ into that home would have changed this father's heart and behavior.

Here's the letter from Alicia:

Amanda,

Heh! How's your day been going? Mine's been OK I think. Do you remember how I called you the first time yesterday? Well, I was freaking out because Dad was drinking and stuff. I guess it wasn't that bad then but it got worse later on.

Mama got home about 6:00 or quarter after last night. She was in Atlanta all day. When she walked into the kitchen I told her that he had been drinking since I got home. Anyway, she just said to stay out of his way and not to get him worked up. Guess what? Melissa and Cody got him worked up!

After we all ate dinner the two little people and I walked off while Mom and Dad were eating. Dad totally went off his rocker! He started slamming dishes around, slamming doors, and throwing chairs around.

Joanie and her mom, and Emily came by about 7:30 last night and I told Emily to leave Mom alone for a minute. She was crying. Emily looked at me and just about cried.

I called you at about 8:30 and "Daddy" (that's me) said you were still at church.

Before that, at about 7:30, I called Jason to come and pick me up over at the elementary school. He came down there and sat and we talked for about 45 minutes. He made me feel a lot better.

This morning, Jason came and picked me up and we went to Henderson Falls Park. We sat and watched the waterfall for a while. Then we walked down the path and played on the playground. McDonald's was on our way to school so we ate breakfast, for once!!

I guess I feel better now. Please do me a favor. Don't say anything to David or if you do, tell him not to say anything to anyone, OK? Don't tell "Daddy" (me) because I don't want him to start worrying about me staying at home. I promise you I will call you to see if I can stay with you guys when I'm having problems OK? Read this.

I, ALICIA, PROMISE . . . That I'll <u>call you</u>!!!!

I told you that I'd write to you and I did. I'm in Coach Beck's class right now and I'm just about bored out of my mind. I guess I'll see you later after school. I've gotta go but I'll try to call you later. Oh yeah! I've gotta go to church tonight too! So I don't know when I'll be home.

Talk to you later. LOVE YA–

Hotrod (Alicia)
P.S. Smile

Amanda and I have always remembered Alicia, even to this day. I still feel very sad for her, but I know she is grown up and has a life of her own now, which thankfully, is separate from her father's abusive ways.

CHAPTER THIRTY-FOUR

FOLLOWING UP AND CHECKING UP

It's wonderful to follow up with folks. I ran into Ralph Singleton about six months ago. His work crew showed up at a house I was working on. He was really looking good and things were going well for him. Somehow, he was much happier with life than he was before. I haven't seen either of the Bobs for several years, and as for David, I see him once in a while. I'm glad I had a positive influence on him and others too.

God has brought some really great people into my life who have followed up with me, as well. I have many good friends at Glad Tidings Assemblies of God, in Toccoa, and I have many friends in the business community that I've come to know and appreciate.

Of course, I appreciate my family, too. They have been close to me through all of this, especially my daughters.

As we look in and check up on each other we need to check up on ourselves. What's the sign of a life on the right track? In a nutshell, it's the strength of our witness for Christ.

Here are some questions we can ask ourselves: have we handled the difficulties of life in a Christian manner? How do people feel about us over time? Are we learning and growing in God? If we've lived obediently under God's guidance, then we'll have a good, strong witness that will stand. Our initial testimony may help win some but our ongoing witness will speak volumes and win many.

My friends and family saw me go through some of the hardest times imaginable, like when my wife and kids disappeared and Deputy, Randy, hounded me with divorce papers. I know I showed fear and anger at times, but overall, with everyone watching, God worked it all out and helped me find strength in Him. I trust *that* has been my witness and testimony.

While my friends and employees were good to me, God was *especially* good to me. My life was falling apart, but God was the glue that kept me together. Even though I'd sometimes lose control, God kept my reputation intact. Folks would say, "Doug, if you hadn't been a Christian, I don't think you ever would have survived." I agreed with them. May I stop right here and say, "Thank You, Lord, Jesus for following through with me. And thank you dear friends, for standing by me. I am truly grateful."

LEARNING TO GIVE UP THE CONTROLS

God has shown me a lot in the midst of my trials. Most importantly, He's shown me how to take my hands off the steering wheel of life. It's an unending struggle, really, but I know if I am going to walk the Christian walk and be a blessing and a true witness for Christ, I have to surrender. I have to stop trying to be in control of everything in my life.

As Christians, how can this be accomplished? Well first, God offers each of us His Holy Spirit. I drew upon the power of God's Holy Spirit who graciously lives inside of me, to keep me from a life of total destruction. He helped me spot my mistakes and showed me how to make more God-centered decisions. And He guided me through the minefields of life. But I had to give up *self* to be victorious. I had to quit resisting the Lord's leading in order to be a conqueror.

Surrender was the key to finding peace at last. And I can tell you, that is *real* freedom. Freedom in Jesus! Only God's power can keep a person's life in line and then, only as long as we let Him call the shots. In that sense, I'm glad to be a prisoner of Jesus Christ. Bondage to Christ is transforming and it offers the greatest freedom on earth and in Heaven. It is a "bondservant's freedom", to serve and worship the One and only Son of God. I have been arrested by His love, and I am a prisoner of His freedom. Hallelujah!

PREJUDICE: I WAS IN THE MINORITY

I John 4:7-8; (KJV)
***Beloved, let us love one another:
for love is of God;
and every one that loveth is born
of God, and knoweth God.
He that loveth not knoweth not God;
for God is love.***

Before I went to prison, I was very prejudiced, but of course, I would never admit that. Then in prison one morning, God really opened my eyes. During headcount, I realized that out of 685 inmates, only 56 of us were white. Suddenly, I wished I'd been born black because now I knew what it was like to be in the minority.

I always thought I was a caring Christian, but after settling into prison life and getting men together for Bible studies, God showed me a different side of black folks; the side I never saw before. I discovered they were just plain old folks like me: some good and some bad but loved by God. He loves us all equally and we need to love others as He does.

God would wake me in the middle of the night and bring revelation to me about things I needed to learn. One morning He whispered deep into my soul,

"Doug, every man has a heart, regardless of their color. Your job is to win that heart to Christ." I came to fully understand what it means to love everyone.

God also gave me a very special burden for prisoners, which He later used in my life. He wanted me to care about all prisoners because each one is so needy for Jesus. There is a heart beating inside each man's breast; therefore, each one can hear about the gracious saving love God has for them.

God isn't hindered by how big or bad or mean a man is. God's pure Word--applied like ointment--can make a man become like a little child; innocent and willing to follow the Spirit of the Lord in faith.

I've seen this happen to some men with a chest size as big as 54", all packed into a little size 44" muscle shirt. (They do it so they can look *b-a-a-a-a-d*.) When God begins dealing with them, they go to their knees and unashamedly weep like three-year-old babies.

God can break in upon men's hearts and bring them to repentance. He brings them to the altar for healing and mending. Afterward, they can stand for the first time in their lives as *real* men. They become sold out to the Lord, lock, stock, and barrel. And by the way, nobody dares to make fun of them, either!

THE BIRTH OF MY PRISON MINISTRY

2 Corinthians 5:17; *(KJV)*
Therefore if any man be in Christ, he is a new creature: old things are passed away; behold, all things are become new.

While I was still behind bars, God gave me a burden for prisoners that grew to the point where He

187

began to separate me from them in a strange and magnificent way. It was like they were the prisoners, and I was the one brought in to help them, living along side of them on a full-time basis. I was actually losing the fear and loneliness I had before. God was lifting it from me like He was taking a dirty shirt off my back.

At times I thought I was just becoming institutionalized. Maybe I was so ingrained in the system that I wanted to be there; things were easier, somehow. This is just what brings so many men and women back. You see, when inmates are released and free again, they're treated badly by those who know where they've been. No one wants to give them a chance. It's hard to start over. They get rejected and discouraged and end up doing something dumb that lands them right back behind bars. With some it's perpetual. They repeat the same mistakes over and over because it's the only life they know. Thankfully, this was definitely not my outlook.

My purpose was to minister to those in need. I knew God could change lives and His power was greater than those needs. But it would require an invitation to do so. And I was there to help show the way. Only Christ has the power to break through the vicious cycle of recidivism. Only Christ can set a person free from it all. Only He can truly change lives.

So my ministry to prisoners really started when the Lord let my heart see needy people in bondage, confined in prison and walled in by degrading sin-- clutched in the grips of utter hopelessness. He then filled me with the desire to bring true hope to each of these men; the hope that can only be found in our eternal Lord and Savior, Jesus Christ.

CHAPTER THIRTY-FIVE

MY DWELLING PLACE

Psalm 91:1; KJV
*He that dwelleth in the secret place
of the most High
shall abide under the shadow
of the Almighty.*

I began to meditate on the Psalms and decided God would be my dwelling place, not these prison cells! I made a sincere commitment to the Lord and asked Him to be my strength. In return, I promised to be obedient to Him, and I began to read His Word and pray every day.

GOD, ME, AND PRAYER

Matthew 12:43-45; (NKJV)
*An Unclean Spirit Returns
When an unclean spirit goes out of a man,
he goes through dry places, seeking rest,
and finds none. Then he says,
'I will return to my house from which I came.'
And when he comes, he finds it empty,
swept, and put in order. Then he goes
and takes with him seven other spirits
more wicked than himself,
and they enter and dwell there;
and the last state of that man
is worse than the first. . .*

I remember that Daniel had been thrown into the lion's den for praying three times a day. Since I was already in the den so-to-speak, I was committed to doing the same thing. I understood that to have a godly life I'd need to really want one. So I wet my desires by making prayer time my first priority each day.

I wanted God to lead me through prayer. That meant I had to spend more time listening than speaking. I asked God to wake me up in the middle of the night so I could have some quality private time with Him. What I asked for in faith, he provided in fact. I had some wonderful times with the Lord!

God revealed many things that were wrong in my life; unconfessed things I had never dealt with before. In the quiet of the night, God would reveal and explore each issue with me, one by one. Then He'd remove them, leaving a *hole* in my inner being. I knew from the Scriptures that I needed protection from any evil that could come into that void, so I prayed God would take each vacant spot and fill me with His precious Holy Spirit.

Walking with God became a more natural part of my everyday life. Prayer was simply my reasonable service to Him, and I found witnessing much, much easier. My cockiness faded away and I was better equipped to walk in love and humility. I was more willing to help and teach others in the ways of God. In short, I became a changed man and other people noticed it even before I did.

I became washed and clean in Jesus. He made me into a brand new creature. The old things were passing away and everything was becoming new. If only I had developed this same quality of relationship when I first met Jesus, I probably wouldn't have taken the path I did that led me to prison. But that's another story in itself, isn't it?

WHAT ABOUT THE OFFERING PLATE?

Trust And Obey
[Words & Music JH Sammis & Daniel B Towner; public domain]

When we walk with the lord,
in the light of His Word
What a glory He sheds on our way
While we do His good will,
He abides with us still
And with all who will trust and obey
Trust and obey, for there's no other way
To be happy in Jesus, but to trust and obey

The Bible says we are to *tithe* by giving ten percent of our income back to God. This is done in order to grow our faith and to show our gratitude for all He's done for us. It's not that God wants our money. It's that God wants our heart. Our heart is usually where our treasure is.

I wanted to give, but I didn't have any income. What was I supposed to do, here behind bars? I asked God how I could keep up with my tithes. He answered my prayers by showing me I could tithe on something other than money. He said, "Isn't it true that you have been given 24 hours each day? Why not give me your focused attention for 2.4 hours of each day?"

I considered the idea and decided to obey God. I proceeded to give Him one-tenth of my time from that moment on. My prayer life grew not only in quality but in frequency. I prayed when I woke up in the morning, then I prayed before each meal, I prayed during our Bible study in the evening, and I prayed before I went to bed. Finally, I prayed during those special times in the middle of the night so I was praying a total of seven times a day. I know that seven is the number of perfection and I felt this was God's *finishing school* for me.

The strength I gained as a result of tithing on my time helped me lead men to Jesus, and to survive prison riots, death threats, and more. Resolving to be a ***"doer of the Word and not just a hearer only"*** (see James 1:22), helped me rise above my circumstances. That's how I reached *the other side of freedom*, even when my physical freedom had been taken away. It was my obedience to His truth that set me free.

I'm still so amazed at how patient God is with me, and with mankind in general. While God has need of nothing, at the same time we have nothing to offer Him. We are completely penniless and worthless. Yet our simple quiet time is more precious to Him than one could say. How dare we keep the owner of the universe waiting. Unbelievable. I was more aware of this with each passing day. Until I was surrendered, I had been so unkind and undone, going on in my own ignorance. Yet God continued to be there for me in a really big way. And as I obeyed Him, I grew in Him.

God was not as concerned about the offering plate, as He was about my willingness to give out of what I didn't have. Here's a poem I found by Richard M. "Pek" Gunn" of Tennessee. It describes what I've been trying to say.

If I
(Richard M. "Pek" Gunn")

If I could go back and undo
some wrongs I've done along the way
And knew the wounds that I've caused
were healed of all the scars today
The steps I've caused someone to take
by thoughtless ways in which I've trod
have led to a confused estate
instead of simple trust in God.
If someone else still wanders on
who followed my unsteady track
and lost the way for lack of light
because my lantern globe was black,
if I could gather up and bind
the wasted years that I have spent
and treat them as they've never been
today I'd be much more content.
I'm pardoned for my undone past
but even so, the hurt is done
for out there somewhere in the dark
a soul is lost I might have won

Now I thank God for every new scrap of
knowledge I can get because everything I learn leads
to growth. I just wish I would have given my whole life
over to the Lord many years earlier. I often bemoan
the years I wasted. I'll never be able to undo them or
redo them. I must, therefore, concentrate on today and
on what is to come. I must remember to continue in
the ways of giving. It's not about what I put in the
offering plate. Rather, it's about the giving of myself in
ways I can, whenever I can. It's been said that the

measure of one's value is equal to what he does for others. May that part of my life be richly and truly blessed.

WHAT IS PROFITABLE?

Matthew 16:26; (KJV)
***For what is a man profited,
if he shall gain the whole world,
and lose his own soul?
or what shall a man give
in exchange for his soul?***

The question is, what price would we be willing to pay to spend our lives in pursuit of worldly ambitions, pleasing only ourselves? In other words, what would it be worth to us, if we could be in charge of our own destiny, instead of investing ourselves into the kingdom of God?

The answer is *nothing*. That's right. Nothing. Nothing is worth hanging on to if it would mean losing God.

I've made poor choices and more poor choices. Many people make excuses for their bad decisions. I had plenty of them. What about you?

Sometimes people even try to justify their mistakes by some contorted use of Scripture. But we need to get the real Word into us and understand what God is saying. Then we need to live by it and stick to it.

God can work with us. He can shape us and mold us into who He has created us to be. But it can only be done if we put Him first and obey His commands. If we will abandon everything that is propping us up and trust in Him, our life will be a beautiful thing. And, we will have gained our souls in the process.

CHAPTER THIRTY-SIX

HOW TO KNOW GOD IS ON YOUR SIDE

Romans 8:28; (KJV)
***And we know that all things work
together for good to them that
love God, to them who are the called
according to his purpose.***

People often say, "Well I goofed up, but it'll all work out somehow. Que Sera Sera. Yes, ***"all things work together for good"***. But the truth is, most people quote this Scripture and end the passage right there. They miss something very important that follows. It's the part that brings God into the picture. Let's read the rest of it.

The next part says, ***"to them that love God"***. This is so overlooked. And there's more. It goes on to say, ***"to them who are the called according to his purpose"***.

So what does it all mean? Here's the key: if you don't love God, He isn't going to do anything for you except keep the fields growing, the rain falling, and the sun shining. Moreover, if you're not *the called* of God, that means you're not *saved* and you're not one of His children. If you're not one of His kids, He's not going to help you.

Think of it this way: as kind-hearted as you might be, would you tell your next door neighbor to move all of his children into your house so you could take care of them for the rest of their natural lives? Of course not! They are not your children.

195

It's the same with God. Unless the Holy spirit nudges your heart and moves you to accept Jesus as your Savior, you won't be born-again which is the only way into God's family. Therefore, **"all things working together for good"** will not apply to you. This promise is only for those who belong to God. Everyone else is strictly on their own!

As for me, I limited God's workings in my life because I wouldn't let Him in. I didn't belong to Him and I lived as an unbeliever. Therefore, God owed me nothing. Had I accepted Jesus as my Lord and Savior, I could have reaped the blessings of being one of His children. Then His strength and power would have been mine for the asking. It could have been my first step toward living a life of freedom and victory. Did you know, you can take that first step if you choose to do so?

I used to long for a wise advisor in my early years. If I had asked Jesus into my life back then I would have had the greatest advisor/counselor in the world. But I waited almost too long, and I missed out on a lot of His protection and help.

Now, I'd like to be *your* advisor; your big brother if you will. Let me say this: don't go through life weak and defenseless. Instead, invite Jesus Christ to come into your heart today. Learn to put Him at the top of your priority list. You'll never regret it. And you'll have the assurance of knowing that God is on your side and He is working all things for your good, because you'll be among the *called*, according to His purpose!

LEARNING TO FOLLOW THE LORD

Here's some advice that's seriously needed today and you would do well to take it to heart. These are the words of Jesus Himself.

Matthew 11:28-30; (KJV)
Come unto me, all ye that labor and
are heavy laden, and I will give you rest.
Take my yoke upon you, and learn of me;
for I am meek and lowly in heart:
and ye shall find rest unto your souls.
For my yoke is easy, and my burden is light.

Jesus will never steer you wrong. He will always be there for you. Don't learn your lessons the hard way like I did. It will only add up to years of heartache.

I spent most of my years digging and scratching and getting nowhere. Eventually, I ended up in prison. There, God gently sat me down with no outside distractions, and lovingly gave me the advice I so desperately needed. It was so simple. But that's just like God. He uses **"simple, foolish things to confound the wise"**, (see I Corinthians 1:27).

How foolish would it be for us to have access to computers, advanced science, and technology, and then not use them to our advantage? It would be like trying to plow a field with a spoon and an old, sickly calf. Yes, the power of God waits for us. He wants us to come to Him. God wants to give us all of His resources that we might be blessed in all we do. But instead, we run off with our little spoon and failing animal to do our own thing.

What's the answer to this whole mess? Follow God! Just do it!! Hindsight is poor-sight. Why not get a little foresight. Remember the simplicity of what Jesus said: "Follow Me."

DRAWING CLOSE TO GOD'S WORD

I Peter 2:2; (KJV)
***As newborn babes, desire the sincere
milk of the word,
that ye may grow thereby . . .***

Hebrews 5:12; (NKJV)
***Spiritual Immaturity
For though by this time you ought to be
teachers, you need someone to teach you
again the first principles of the oracles
of God; and you have come
to need milk and not solid food.***

Prior to being in prison I had never read the Scriptures completely through. Without having that knowledge I was like a man trying to fight my battles alone while standing on one leg. So I decided the day after my pre-trial that I would make a commitment to really get into the Word. Here's what I wrote in my Bible.

***Saturday, September 14th, 1985
(11th wedding anniversary)
I will read God's Word from
beginning to end THIS YEAR!***

I guess I was like so many other people who are saved. They think, "Well, I've done my part; I've accepted Jesus. Now I'm saved. The rest is up to God. He'll take care of me, feed me, and when I get soiled from brushing up against the world He will bath me and put me back into good standing until I need His help again." That kind of thinking is alright when you're a baby Christian, but eventually, a person has to grow up in the Lord and move on to maturity.

After I was saved, I had a lot of growing to do. For one thing, vanity had been a major motivator in my life, even as a church worker. I reaped some reward for my efforts but I should have been focused as a dedicated follower of Christ, laying up my treasure in Heaven.

Here's some great advice from the apostle, Paul. If we heed his words we'll see a big difference in our life.

Philippians 2:13-16; (KJV).
**For it is God which worketh in you
both to will and to do of his good pleasure.
Do all things without murmurings
and disputings: That ye may be
blameless and harmless,
the sons of God, without rebuke,
in the midst of a crooked and perverse nation,
among whom ye shine as lights in the world;
Holding forth the word of life;
that I may rejoice in the day of Christ,
that I have not run in vain,
neither labored in vain.**

I think that attaining maturity is an ongoing process, and studying the Scriptures with all of its warnings and advice is central to that. As we read God's word and meditate on His truths, we are actually renewing our mind; we're changing our thinking into what it ought to be. That, in turn, will change the course of our entire life. If we'll only do our part, God will step in and do the rest.

CHAPTER THIRTY-SEVEN

GOD SPEAKS AGAINST WHAT'S UNNATURAL

Romans 1:24-32; (KJV).
*Wherefore God also gave them up to
uncleanness through the lusts of
their own hearts, to dishonour
their own bodies between themselves:
Who changed the truth of God into a lie,
and worshipped and served the creature
more than the Creator,
who is blessed for ever. Amen.
For this cause God gave them up
unto vile affections: for even their women
did change the natural use into that which is
against nature: And likewise also the men,
leaving the natural use of the woman,
burned in their lust one toward another;
men with men working that which is unseemly,
and receiving in themselves that recompense
of their error which was meet. And even
as they did not like to retain God in their
knowledge, God gave them over
to a reprobate mind, to do those things
which are not convenient; Being filled with all
unrighteousness, fornication, wickedness,
covetousness, maliciousness;
full of envy, murder, debate, deceit,
malignity; whisperers, Backbiters, haters of God,
despiteful, proud, boasters, inventors of evil
things, disobedient to parents, Without
understanding, covenant breakers,
without natural affection, implacable,*

unmerciful: Who knowing the judgment of God,
that they which commit such things
are worthy of death,
not only do the same, but have
pleasure in them that do them.

I not only read this but I meditated on this passage. I realized God wanted me to understand things from His point of view so I could help others. It was very important for me to become more and more grounded in various subjects, and this subject related well to prison life.

GOD SPEAKS ABOUT WHAT HE REQUIRES

Romans 1:16-22; *(KJV).*
For I am not ashamed of the gospel
of Christ: for it is the power of God
unto salvation to every one
that believeth; to the Jew first,
and also to the Greek.
For therein is the righteousness of God
revealed from faith to faith: as it is written,
The just shall live by faith.
For the wrath of God is revealed
from heaven against all ungodliness and
unrighteousness of men,
who hold the truth in unrighteousness;
Because that which may be known of God
is manifest in them; for God hath shewed it
unto them. For the invisible things of him
from the creation of the world are
clearly seen, being understood by the things
that are made, even his eternal power
and Godhead; so that they are without excuse:

> *Because that, when they knew God,*
> *they glorified him not as God, neither were*
> *thankful; but became vain in their imaginations,*
> *and their foolish heart was darkened.*
> *Professing themselves to be wise,*
> *they became fools . . .*

God was really talking to me through this Scriptures one day. I read it through carefully, then flipped the page over to continue. Suddenly I was overwhelmed with delight. There in the page margin, I spotted some handwriting. It was something my little girl, Amanda, must have written some time ago while we were sitting in church together. It very simply said:

"I love my daddy."

I began to cry and pray: "God, I'm so sorry that I don't have the same kind of love and commitment to you that my sweet baby girl has for me. I can never be a godly example to my children unless I start loving You freely and openly from my heart, just like my sweet child has done. Help me God, to learn more about the kind of love that sacrifices so that I might overcome my selfishness and learn to give and to care and to show mercy. Help me let the old self die, never to rise again that I might always say, 'Not I but Christ be honored, loved, and exalted in everything I do'."

Up to this point, I still had one ear open to certain men who wanted to persuade me to manipulate my way out of prison by eliciting sympathy in the courtroom. And they wanted to help me get back at my wife for slamming me into this place. They even suggested I might *do away* with her. I heard all the tricks of the trade and had many offers to work out my revenge.

Then one morning at breakfast, I bowed my head to give thanks for my food, and my friend, J.C., made it very clear that I was to start becoming a doer of the word and not a speaker of it only. God wasn't interested in that kind of a walk. J.C. gave me the following scripture to think about.

**"But be ye doers of the word,
and not hearers only,
deceiving your own selves,"** (James 1:22)

Through this admonishment, God convicted me about speaking out of both sides of my mouth. On the one hand I was professing to be a Christian, but on the other hand, I was considering the deceptive advice offered by those who were "of the world, and not of God". That's what J.C. was talking about. The so-called forgiveness I had claimed toward my wife was just lip service. Here I was trying to tell others how to act when at the same time, I couldn't get my own act together. I was shooting off my mouth while taking advantage of all the loopholes concocted by fellow inmates. What kind of a witness was that?

J.C. really put it to me. He asked, "What does God require of you? Honesty." That did it. There was no way I could ever hope to be a witness for Jesus without that. No, I certainly wasn't ashamed of the Gospel of Christ, but I no longer wanted to be ashamed of myself either.

James 2:8-14: (NKJV).
**If you really fulfill the royal law
according to the Scripture,
"You shall love your neighbor as yourself,"
you do well; but if you show partiality,
you commit sin, and are convicted**

> *by the law as transgressors.*
> *For whoever shall keep the whole law,*
> *and yet stumble in one point, he is guilty of all.*
> *For He who said, "Do not commit adultery,"*
> *also said, "Do not murder."*
> *Now if you do not commit adultery,*
> *but you do murder,*
> *you have become a transgressor of the law.*
> *So speak and so do as those who will be*
> *judged by the law of liberty. For judgment*
> *is without mercy to the one*
> *who has shown no mercy.*
> *Mercy triumphs over judgment.*

MY MAFIA FRIEND

I have to tell you about a guy I met--a Mafia boss--that I managed to make friends with, (who shall remain unnamed). Even in prison, he was powerful and operated through a number of hardened mafia soldiers he had around him. He sent word to me, through one of his men:

"Hey preacher, *The Boss* wants to see you." I want you to know I had some anxious moments over that. What could he want from me?

It turns out, The Boss had heard about my holding Bible studies on the ranges and he wanted me to get him a Bible. So I did. He appreciated that so much that he offered to take care of *a little matter* for me, namely, my wife. There it was again: supreme temptation, right in my face. All I had to do was say the word and I could have had all the revenge I wanted.

The Boss offered to have drugs planted in her car and then have her stopped. The drugs would have been found and she would have been convicted of possession.

He also offered to have her kidnaped, pumped full of drugs, and sold across the border into Mexico as a prostitute. There were several other equally heinous ideas he had for her. I'm so thankful God had already been dealing with me about it all before I was tempted to act. Otherwise, I might have accepted one of the offers. I'm so glad it didn't happen. Instead, God led me to forgive Nora and love her the way a Christian husband should, even though she put me in prison.

So I told The Boss, "No thanks," and went back to my own cell. Several more times he offered to repay me, but I always humbly declined. I thanked him just the same and maintained my good witness before this mafia kingpin. But I must give all the credit and glory to God. The power of His Word was at work in my life and I was living by it.

The book of James was the perfect prescription for me at the time. Of course, that was no coincidence. I wanted to have a godly nature, just like the Bible described, so I made sure I surrendered myself before the cross each day. And I committed myself to being a doer of the Word, not a hearer only, just like J.C. had explained.

To the best of my ability, I made sure all my dealings with other people were done in humility. Finally, I submitted myself to the *potter's house* daily, to be broken and rebuilt anew. In turn, God was turning me into a useful vessel. When I understood what was required of me, I quit praying my old prayer, "Lord, get me out of here." Instead, I got down to the business of praying for my wife, and, asking God to show me what He wanted me to do in this place where Hell and humanity had so recklessly collided.

CHAPTER THIRTY-EIGHT

SUFFER THE LITTLE CHILDREN

After our two-year-old daughter died in the dam break at Toccoa Falls College, we had this Scripture put on her headstone.

Mark 10:14; (KJV).
[Jesus said:] Suffer the little children to come unto me, and forbid them not: for of such is the kingdom of God.

Every time I hear of parents abusing their children I think of this verse. How can they do it?

In the past, I had been guilty of being a bit rough on my children. No, I wasn't abusive but I was a disciplinarian; even strict and domineering. But there's a limit to what a normal father should and should not do.

For years, I raised my family in a way I thought was loving, kind, and gentle. But out of concern, I think I was too strict. I would spank my kids to correct them but I was also quite hard on their self-esteem. I have no joy in admitting that. I've tried to apologize as best as I could, and have put it all under the blood of Christ. Carrying that on my chest all the time was very hard to bear. I'm so grateful for forgiveness.

There's another kind of abuse: neglect. And I neglected to care if my family went to church or not. It was always an on-again-off-again thing with me. If it was a special occasion we might go, but all too often the family went without me while I rode around on my motorcycle. That was my big Sunday thrill.

Sometimes I'd persuade them to go riding with me because it was a lot of fun. We'd all ride dirt bikes, or, my wife and I would go out on bigger bikes for a short road trip. I figured that after working hard all week, I deserved it. In retrospect, I wonder how much of my marriage failed as a result. And it burdens me to think that my kids may have come to the Lord a lot sooner if I had kept them in church under the teaching of God's word.

I offered my family all the freedom in the world to do what they wanted to do, even on Sundays. I felt that I was being a pretty good Dad. Sadly though, neither my goodness or theirs will get them into Heaven. We need to suffer the little children to come unto Jesus. For if we

***Train up a child in the way he should go: ...
when he is old, he will not depart from it,***
(Proverbs 22:6; KJV).

DYSFUNCTIONAL LOVE

Throughout my life, I've had a tremendous need for someone to love me. I've always been a very loving person, yet the enigma about me was that I was strict and controlling. It caused people to push away and withhold the love I so desperately needed. The farther they drifted, the more I'd pull them in, tightening the cords. I was so afraid of losing them.

As a kid, I badly needed my daddy's love but I never felt I received it. I guess that hurt my "love relationships" in my adult life. What I ended up with was a kind of dysfunctional love. It was a love that didn't work. It was grounded in need and anxiety instead of freedom and peace.

Sometimes the person trying to love me had it all wrong too. They might have been self-centered or needy in their own way but I usually didn't figure that out until time had passed. In the meanwhile, I was deceived. Satan is the master of deceit you know. He loves to wreak havoc in this area of people's lives. And we are often taken off guard because love is something we all really need.

People all over the world are searching for real love, but the only place it can be found is in Jesus. His love is complete, perfect, fulfilling, and selfless. We need to get ourselves grounded in His love. Then we'll be in a better position to receive love from others, even if it's not perfect. Once we've been filled by the love of Christ, human love will have a secondary place in our heart.

Chasing after the wrong kind of love brings nothing but pain. Dysfunctional love can put a person in the worst prison of all. It only produces broken friendships, broken marriages and homes, and even addictions and prostitution. But when we have the love of God, we can walk in the fruit of the spirit: peace, joy, patience, kindness, compassion, understanding, and real love! This is the abundant life God promised His children, and it can be ours if we'll just reach for it.

THE THREE KINDS OF LOVE

The Bible says there are three kinds of love: there is caring love, sensual love, and godly love. Caring love is referred to as "Philao" in the original language of the New Testament. Generally speaking, it's the love among family and close friends. It's a sharing kind of love that is common to everyone and operates on the two-way street of give-and-take.

"Eros" or sensual love is born in the hearts of a men and a woman. "Eros" love says, "if it feels good, do it". This love is actually quite selfish because it's given with the expectation of receiving. We give away our heart but we are motivated by our real desire to receive the same kind of love back. This kind of love can imprison people. It seems real but actually, it's a false love and so people get trapped.

The third kind of love is called "Agape" love. It goes above and beyond all the other types of love. It carries a special ingredient called *forgiveness*. Without forgiveness, one can never resolve a damaged relationship that might otherwise end up in divorce. "Agape" love can prevent divorce.

Furthermore, "Agape" love is a "one-way-giving" kind of love. It usually costs the giver, and it is done without expecting to receive anything in return. Jesus was a true model for "Agape" love. He gave it at the cost of His life. He did it for you and me so we could gain eternal life. He paid the price in full, for us. He offered Himself to all of humanity for the forgiveness of our sins. It's our choice as to whether we will receive His love or reject Him.

I've experienced each of these kinds of love in my life. My friend Ralph showed me a "Philao" kind of love. He cooked for me and helped me back to health. He cared for me in a brotherly way.

Unfortunately, I experienced the "Eros" kind of love when I began to meet women. I often mistook it for more than what it was. "Eros" is part of the gift God gives to a man and a woman within the bounds of marriage. But marriages based on "Eros" alone will not last long. This is one of the reasons so many marriages fail. There has to be more than sensuality. It takes much more than that to sustain a marriage relationship.

The strength of a marriage is equal only to the amount of "Agape" love that is exchanged. When a marriage is God-centered and sacrificial, it can then become a never-ending marriage. Both parties will be in it "until death do us part." Only "Agape" love is strong enough to overcome the many bumps in the road that a marriage will encounter through the years.

How can people fill their lives and their marriages with "Agape" love? By surrendering their hearts and lives to Christ. It's a daily process, and if done faithfully, will open the way for the Holy Spirit to not only indwell us but direct us through the challenges of life we face each day.

If you have "Agape" love to give, you have a gift more precious than a diamond ring. Sensual, "Eros" love is like a stone tied around your neck. You can drown in it. Don't trade your diamond for a stone.

Also, test the type of love that's being offered to you. Compare it with the cross of Christ. If it doesn't measure up, drop it. Use Christ as your model and stay out of the prison of false love. Test the love you're being offered. Look for God's kind of love in it. If it's there, accept it and then give it away to others.

CHAPTER THIRTY-NINE

OUR DECISIONS INFLUENCE OTHERS

Our lives and the lives we touch are forever affected by our decisions, whatever they may be. Remember, we are responsible for every person we influence and the consequence is often eternal. We need to let God control our relationships. It will bring peace in the end, (rather than sorrow which is what happened to me).

We need to give God our best efforts in everything and let Him do the rest. Sharing our best with others is sharing something very precious indeed.

As Christians, we can not live as we please and at the same time please the God of agapé love who lives within us. Only a God-honoring life will satisfy.

God asks two things of us: first, to love the Lord God with all our heart, and second, to love our neighbor as our self. Living by these two commandments will have a profound influence on everything else in our lives.

God had to get me alone in a prison cell where He could have my undivided attention before I would learn these things. While there, I read the Bible all the way through and learned many valuable lessons. Oh, how I wish I had started years earlier. Instead, I went my own rebellious way and brought about a lot of suffering. Thank You, Lord for never giving up on me. It's just another reason I love you so much today!

ALL IT TAKES IS ONE

Acts 16:25-34; (KJV).
***And at midnight Paul and Silas prayed,
and sang praises unto God: and the prisoners
heard them. And suddenly there was a great
earthquake, so that the foundations
of the prison were shaken:
and immediately all the doors were opened,
and every one's bands were loosed.
And the keeper of the prison awaking
out of his sleep, and seeing the prison doors
open, he drew out his sword, and would have
killed himself, supposing that the prisoners
had been fled. But Paul cried with a loud voice,
saying, Do thyself no harm: for we are all here.
Then he called for a light, and sprang in,
and came trembling, and fell down before Paul
and Silas, And brought them out,
and said, Sirs, what must I do to be saved?
And they said, Believe on the Lord Jesus Christ,
and thou shalt be saved, and thy house.
And they spake unto him the word of the Lord,
and to all that were in his house. And he took
them the same hour of the night, and washed
their stripes; and was baptized, he and all his,
straightway. And when he had brought them
into his house, he set meat before them,
and rejoiced, believing in God
with all his house.***

Here's a wonderful example of how one person became saved, and then led his entire household likewise.

After the dam break, my own family saw how much my life had changed. As a result, many of my thirteen brothers and sisters came to the Lord and were saved, along with family members too. God drew them in through the survivors' testimonies. They saw that in the midst of this tragedy, the survivors kept their unwavering faith in God. It was a testimony of God's care for us, his children. (For stories about other families who went through the dam break, see *Dam Break In Georgia*.)

While I was in prison, I was aware that some of my children were not yet saved. That was difficult for me to take. Seeing my sons and daughters outside of the family of God was disheartening. But I didn't give up. I've always said that if God can save someone as bad as me, I know He can save the rest of my family. There's always hope!

Eventually, I did manage to get it together for the sake of my family. Then blessings spilled over from me to others. Take the girl who wrote that letter to my daughter. Her Father had her trapped. He was controlled by the power of Satan through his disobedience and his use of alcohol. By the time the girl came into our lives, she could see the difference between our spiritual life and the one her father forced upon her. Even in her abusive situation, she saw Jesus as her answer; she found freedom in Jesus Christ. She accepted Christ as her Savior and crossed over to the other side of freedom. If you know someone like that, pray for them, love them, and witness to them about what God has done for you. God will use you to bring them into a personal relationship with Him.

How are things in your household today? It only takes one person to initiate change. Why not set the example and lead the way. Why not ask Jesus to come into your heart right now. Ask Him to reveal Himself to you, and tell Him which prison has you bound. He'll set you free if you want Him to. Then give God control of your new freedom. Let Him build you a new life. You can have His assurance. He will forgive your sins: past, present, and future. You will have a brand new beginning in Christ, and in your household too.

If you already are a Christian, then how is your witness? Are there people in your life you've neglected to share Jesus with? Is it because you're lacking in your own spirituality?

If I had it to do over again, things would definitely be different. I would have lived for Christ much sooner.

I challenge you to search yourself to see whether you are hindering your family and friends, or helping them. Don't be cold and indifferent. Unless you take your family into your heart and get as concerned over their spiritual welfare as you are over their worldly needs, you may be building a prison for them.

The Scripture says, **"But seek ye first the kingdom of God, and his righteousness; and all these things shall be added unto you,"** (Matthew 6:33; KJV).

Let God be the key to your happiness, not the worldly jailor who cares only about happenings and possessions. Can you enjoy life? Of course, you can! But you have to look at your priorities and get them in line with God's Word. If you have to be the first one to get up and do something, then do it! It only takes one to start a movement, and you'll never be sorry you did. That pursuit will keep you free of worldly wants and heartbreaks.

GOD TAKES US THROUGH

Psalm 23:4; (KJV).
***Yea, though I walk through the valley
of the shadow of death, I will fear no evil:
for thou art with me; thy rod and thy staff
they comfort me.***

I don't need any greater assurance in this lifetime than to know that God is with me. Whatever else happens, in spite of any trouble near or far, I know my Lord, God is in charge of everything, and that's O.K. with me.

Furthermore, it's not only *in* the valley of the shadow of death that God walks with me but *through* it. That's what the verse actually says.

There have been many valleys in my lifetime, and I'm sure there will yet be more. But I won't be stuck in them. God will take me through, no matter what life has to dish out.

Between the years 1985 and 1986, I was in a valley called Allegheny County Prison, and out of that valley came this book: *Dancing With The Devil On The Other Side Of Freedom.* God birthed several ministries through that experience. How did this happen? God took me through the dance-halls of Hell, and I found my self on the other side.

Reading God's Word was one of the ways I found victory. Chapter 119 in the Book of Psalms is the longest book in the Bible. With its 176 verses, it could be a holy book all by itself. As I read through the Bible while serving my time, this chapter alone was one of the major forces that changed my life.

I've been through the valley of dry bones. I've been through the valley of death. I've been through the valley of unrest and indecision. I've also been on the mountain top, but I have to say that going through the valleys has taught me many valuable lessons. More so than any mountain-top experience ever could have. It was during those difficult times that I really learned how to draw close to God. That's where I found myself on the other side of freedom; the good side; the true-freedom side. That's when I knew I would dance with the devil, no more.

YOUR OPINION COUNTS!

If you have enjoyed this book,
please consider
**writing a short book review
at Amazon.com**
Help us spread the word,
and share Jesus with others too!

www.ingramcontent.com/pod-product-compliance
Lightning Source LLC
LaVergne TN
LVHW011223080426
835509LV00005B/278